WHEN I CAME

TO ENGLAND

D1465189

An Oral History of Life
in 1950s & 1960s Britain

The West Indians

Life, love and lifestyle...
a long way from home

Z. NIA REYNOLDS

WHEN I CAME TO ENGLAND
Copyright 2014
Z. Nia Reynolds
ISBN: 978-0-9540387-2-4
First published in the UK, 2001
Black Stock Photo-Press
This edition: published 2014
Black Stock Books
Black Stock Media
Email:
blackstockmedia@gmail.com
The Oral History Project:
Email: oralstory@yahoo.co.uk
Printed in England.

Cover design: Sarah Edwards
Images: ©Black Stock Photos
Cover photo: Annette Williams
Courtesy of Donald Hinds.

DEDICATION

For Buzz Johnson
A man of vision & purpose

He spent his life freeing
the voices of such as these.

By the ship-load,
by the plane-load...
everybody future plan,
is to get a big-time job;
and settle in the Motherlan'.

— *Louise Bennett*
Colonialisation in Reverse

CONTENTS

FLAMINGO

OCTOBER 1964 2/-

IN THIS ISSUE

DOES **MILLIE** TALK TOO MUCH?

RACHMANISM TODAY

REPORT FROM JAMAICA

INTRODUCTION
By Z. Nia Reynolds

Full of the hope and audacity of dreamers, many West Indians who came to Britain in the 1950s and '60s felt certain that they were coming to a "Motherland"; a place of fair play, opportunity and prosperity.

However, the illusion was soon shattered for some of them, who, instead of encountering a welcoming matriarch, discovered instead a twisted stepmother; the antithesis of any maternal ideal they had imagined.

Colonialism had so perfectly conditioned these people of African descent to see themselves, not as Africans in exile, but as offsprings of Britainnia: "Children" of the British Empire, and Britain: their Mother Land.

The subsequently frosty reception — and not just from the weather — that the vast majority received, was a massive culture shock and served as a wake up call to what it would mean to survive in a strange and, at times, hostile land.

In theory, the arrangement was that post-war Britain needed rebuilding and the newcomers would provide labour. Of course, for some, there was always the implied incentive of "deferred gratification" with its promise of inevitable success for those prepared to graft.

In the majority of cases, they came with a game plan to work hard and get rich; or to at least to get some skills, a trade, employment and enough money to "go back home". Some are still in a kind of shocked state that they are still here some 50, 60 or more years later and that prosperity, like the fair Motherland, is still an illusion.

Work and prospects were the original defining features of the journey: people came expecting to play their part, contribute, follow their dreams and make a life. They did not expect rejection, dejection, and shattered dreams, but stayed on anyway, adjusted their plans, survived and even thrived — in spite of everything.

And, whether they worked for the transport services, civil service, hospitals or factories, often doing jobs scorned by indigenous workers, the investment of their labour, talents and energies helped to make Britain more prosperous, brighter, and more stable.

Looking back at the archive footage or reading the newspaper reports about the arrivants and seeing those fresh-faced, dapper, sharp-suited men and the elegant (if inappropriately-dressed) ladies, engenders a sense of intrigue and pride. *Who are those gorgeous people and what is their story?*

Their arrival heralded a kind of cultural revolution, while the prevailing sense of British froidure was probably expected to induce them to make an about turn and hotfoot it back to their countries. However, it is to their great credit that they overcame the many obstacles in their way, raised their families and strove to make a better life.

Their stories deserve to be told, as honestly and openly as possible, without fear, revision or bias, and who better to tell it than they themselves? As has been noted, the full account of how that generation adapted and survived has yet to be told in great detail. This volume of testimonies, now in its second edition, is a small drop in an ocean of "living memories".

When I Came to England accompanies an exhibition, complete with iconic West Indian living room installation (with its Blue Spot radiogram and paraffin heater, antimacassars, flying ducks and *"Christ is the Head of This House"* plaques), against a soundtrack of oral testimonies merging with music from the period to provide an evocative trip down memory lane.

Documenting the oral experiences of this generation is timely — if not overdue — for numerous reasons: this generation is advancing in years and many have passed away (including some contributors to the first edition, but it seems only right to keep their stories intact: "Age shall not weary them").

Many others have returned to their homelands or have relocated elsewhere, although countless others now call this country "home".

Among the number of those who have passed away are stalwarts of the community who made an impression with their activism, including Len Garrison, John la Rose, Len Dyke and Dudley Dryden, of the legendary Dyke and Dryden haircare brand, Geraldine Connor, Trevor Carter, Ben Bousquet, Syd Burke, Lord Pitt, Bernie Grant, Lord Kitchener. Sadly, the list goes on.

This group of post-war immigrants, mostly ordinary people who did an extraordinary thing in "colonising England in reverse", were nuanced but rather unique, and their passing is the passing of an era. It is therefore important to provide, for posterity, a record of their experiences. Yet, if one turns to the regular history books, it is as though they never even existed.

Their experiences make interesting, at times, inspiring

or even painful reading, particularly in today's Britain where words like, "equal opportunity", "racial equality" and "diversity" are taken for granted, although the struggle to achieve these human rights was fiercely fought over many decades— and still continues.

"What happens to a dream deferred?", asked Langston Hughes in his iconic poem written in the 1920s. That question could and perhaps should be asked in relation to the heritage and legacy of this generation which has become known in soundbite as "The Windrush Generation", a term loved and loathed in equal measure; loathed, not least because it gives the completely false impression that Black people have only been in Britain since 1948 with the arrival of the Windrush, when in fact they have been in Britain since Roman times, and perhaps even before.

The issue of what happened to the "dream deferred" is a fitting question to ask, particularly against the backdrop of an alarming tide of destruction involving Black young men in Britain, who are at once the disproportionate victims and perpertrators of violence.

Those who came to England in the war and post-war years could not in their nightmares have imagined that it could come to this. After all, they went to the "front-line", literally and figuratively: enduring the worse jobs, living conditions and outrageous slurs so that the future generations would not have to.

On top of that, they *had* to prove the likes of Enoch Powell wrong (see *Two Days in April*, p.174).. *So, what went wrong?* That, perhaps, is for another book, another time, although I cannot help thinking that if more young people knew this much about their grand- and great grand-parents' lives and about their roots, struggles, sacrific-es, and efforts, then their own lives and communities would be more positive and progressive. No doubt that will be dismissed as too idealistic and unrealistic, but it's a thought, and I'm convinced of it. In fact, it's my manifesto.

In the meantime, these are real stories and experiences of migration, relocation and transition. They speak of hope, pain, ambition, disappointment, success, frustration, struggle and, at times, of real fire-in-the-belly determination.

And somewhere too there is joy. A joy that passes understanding.

FOREWORD

A NATION IN EXILE
By Donald Hinds

A fair amount of reminiscences of the early years of West Indian migration to Britain are now coming into the public domain, unlike thirty or more years ago. There was a reluctance on the part of those who came to talk about the reasons for, and the experiences of, their being in Britain.

This I know from my days as a reporter on the *West Indian Gazette* (1958-1964) under the editorship of the dynamic Claudia Jones, and my own researches (1964-1966) for my book *Journey To an Illusion* which was published by Heinemann in 1966. People were reluctant to go on record, as if they were protective of their relationship with Britain.

Perhaps they considered interviews as the prerogative of actors and politicians. Now, in the age of television and instant news from distant places, there is a willingness to talk and to record their experiences. It is a revival of an age old custom.

Quite apart from the romance of our African forefathers and mothers being the wise elders of the villages, I recall the old men of my village talking about that other migration as they slapped dominoes on the rum bar counter with great passion.

That migration took them to the farthest shores of the Caribbean Sea and the Gulf of Mexico, like the first inhabitants, the Arawaks and the Caribs. They would talk about their experiences in Cuba, Panama and Costa Rica. They still had their Colon suits and their Panama hats which they wore at weddings and funerals.

The superb reminiscences in this collection will not be found in mainstream history books. Allowing them to be recorded onto the printed page is, in fact, the preservation of an important part of our heritage. The owners of these stories are handing down a priceless legacy to posterity.

As I read them I remembered those cold grey mornings when, as one of the early Black bus conductors employed by London Transport, I pointed out possible places of employment. Some wanted the Telephone Manufacturing Factory, which was located along Effra Road in Brixton, south London, and others wanted PB Cow, the rubber manufacturing company at Streatham Common, and other firms too numerous to list here.

I recall the dark figures with hunched shoulders and damp nostrils, wondering if they would ever feel the hot sun on their faces again.

These stories are the more important because they are the life experiences of ordinary people. They did not pretend to be students, recording artistes, writers and leaders of their people. They came, got low paid jobs, lived in single rooms, brought up their families and, in some cases, saw the dream of returning to the islands fade away.

All human experiences are in these stories. You will feel angry for Mildred who came up to be married only to find out that her boyfriend had another woman; will feel the hopelessness of Samuel when he tried to redeem his three pounds deposit for a room; and will not miss Byron's humour:

> I observed people sunning themselves. Well, they still do that. Obviously they weren't accustomed to a lot of sun so they were making use of the little they got.

One of the pitfalls of oral history is that history will be told to suit the mood of the time. Most people ignore the mistrust that one islander bore towards another, but fifty or so years on and something peculiar has taken place. A significant proportion of the younger generation has grandparents from more than one of the island states.

And, although, nowadays, the term "West Indian" is hardly used (rather, there is the so-called politically correctness of "Afro-Caribbean" and "Black British"), there is West Indian / Caribbean pride among the migrants of the post-immigration years and their descendants which is now generating enough passion to sustain nationhood. Even if it is in voluntary exile.

Donald Hinds is the author of Journey To an Illusion, about West Indians in Britain, first published by Heinemann in 1966. He was a Journalist on the West Indian Gazette newspaper (1958-64), which was edited by the remarkable civil rights activist, Claudia Jones.

"Come see me and come live
with me are two different things."

— *Caribbean saying*

FRED ELLIS

Travelled from the island of St. Vincent on a Spanish boat, "The Irpina", which docked in Plymouth on cold April morning in 1956.

The atmosphere was lousy, the place dark and smoggy. Never would I have imagined that England looked like this: the houses were huddled together and all looking the same.

I wondered what I had let myself in for and I knew that I was going to have to be strong if I was to stay here. What had made me come in the first place was intrigue. I had always wanted to travel and to see this "Great" Britain, so when my friends started leaving the island it spurred me on.

I lived at first in Holloway, north London, with an uncle. It was just one room and you had to share all the facilities and cook on the landing. I got a job two days after arriving here, working at British Rail. I did really want to do book-keeping, that is what I had been trained in, but I couldn't get a job in that field.

The first salary I collected was just over £5.0.0*, which rose to £6.0.0 after some months. With those wages, you could buy £3.0.0 worth of shopping and not be able to eat it all for a fortnight. On top of that, you would send money home, and use some for entertaining, although I was not one for gallivanting. House parties, yes, otherwise, no.

As far as fancying English girls went, well, anyone would fancy them because there were so few black women around; very few compared to the men. Like the other fellows, I would chat girls up, mostly the Irish girls because the English girls weren't so friendly and they hardly used to wash; they always smelled milky. And, remember, in those days, most people didn't have indoor baths, they used to have the communal baths where they had to pay to go.

Also, when we came, many people were walking bare-foot and many parts of London were very run down. It's not an exaggeration to say that we taught English people how to live life. We came here and met with people who were worse off than we were, although I thought we were poor coming from the Caribbean. Their food was mainly bread and dripping and they hardly even went to the seaside. Hygiene was very low.

We were getting attacks from the Teddy Boys but the Jamaicans always stood up for us fellow blacks, regardless of which island we were from. That's one thing: the Jamaicans always had a reputation for sticking up for themselves. It isn't spoken of much but we black people had a hell of a time even sitting in the front of a bus – that created problems, but the Jamaicans paved the way to end that foolishness.

We were forced to buy our own houses and then white people began to get jealous. Our hands were forced into buying, plus we did the menial jobs which they didn't want but they became very resentful. We built this country.

I remember applying for a job at the Overseas Tele-graph Service in the city. The first thing they asked me was if I could use a telephone. I told them "Yes". Then, I had to go into a room, put on headphones and listen while the interviewer dictated something. I had to write down what he said. When he started talking, I missed a word and asked him what he'd said.

He told me, "Write down what you think I said."

From that point, I knew I hadn't got the job, although they had plenty of vacancies.

Another common thing that used to happen is that if you talked to someone on the 'phone they would tell you there were vacancies, but when you got there the gateman wouldn't let you in to talk to the manager. He would tell you there were no jobs going and turn you away. We had to learn to bypass that gateman.

* The old monetary system of pounds, shillings and pence.

Fred, also known as Frank, was awarded an MBE for his services to his community in north London spanning more than 35 years, in the Queen's New Year's Honours Awards in 2012.

WHITFIELD JONES

Retired railway worker. He came from Barbados in 1956.

I was excited because I had never seen so many white people, you know, to me all of them looked alike, at the time. It took me a long time before I could distinguish them by their features. I think they used to say the same about us, too, in those days. Now, I think they've grown to identify us regardless of what colour we are.

I was a carpenter back home and when I came here, I joined the British Railways as a carpenter. One thing, when I was a carpenter at home I always worked for reputable firms, so work was consistent.

So, as fate would have it, when I came here I got to understand that the railways employment was consistent as long as you didn't fight or steal anything from the railways. That was a great asset with me because I am a disciplinarian.

Coming to England in those days was a kind of

fashion. John Brown: gone, your other friend: gone, and you found out, well, you hadn't got many friends home now, so then you come (to England) too. But, I didn't like it much because they used to give us a breakdown of the pay in England: your rent, what you would have to pay for food, and then they would pinpoint that there was not much left for your family at home. You see, but still it was the fashion.

The Italian liners were getting rich transporting people and they were advertising on radio: so many jobs going in Italy, so many jobs going in England. Before I came I never had an impression of England at all, barring what little geographical terms I might have read at school. To think about it, though, if anyone had told me when I was a youngster that in 1956 I'd be in England, I would have said, "You're talking out of your head!"

There wasn't a genuine possibility of going abroad. But, then, after the war, there was all this shortage of employment here and when they had to get emigrants from the West Indies. People from many countries came here for work.

When I first came here I found a couple of boys from Jamaica who used to talk about the summer. And, when they talked about the summer I wasn't hearing about the cold. I thought there must be a summer if they were talking about it, but, on the whole, the weather was so wet and foggy you didn't know what summer they were talking about until that summer came.

I mean, the weather was deadly, really and truly deadly. Take clothes on the line: you'd put them out to dry and they'd be all hard and frozen. Then again, very few people needed a fridge because you could make jello and put it on the window-sill to set, it was so cold. After a time the body would acclimatise to the conditions.

The best experience is that I was fortunately employed in one consistent job. Discrimination was there but I didn't go looking for it. I wanted to get on, you know, to survive, that was it. I am now retired, and I think I've earned it.

The worse experience I had in this country was that in those days you used to live in rooms. I think it was by the mercies of God that I survived, because there was a time when it was very dense and foggy, and people sometimes would have to use a torch-light. In those times, people had their rooms and they had just one toilet in the house. Some people would have a utensil (chamber pot) for their own personal use.

The cost of living was very cheap: five pounds of potatoes for a shilling; you could get a room to live in for two pound ten, that's for a double room. It might have been twenty-five bob for a single room. It would take a long time to save and some people joined Partners* to collect enough money to send for their wives or girlfriends, as the case may be.

Things have changed immensely, really, because sometimes it fascinates me when I pass these supermarket stores and see so many coloured people manning those tills. In previous times you wouldn't find a West Indian fortunate enough to get a job inside those supermarkets serving at the tills.

I think the first one I saw was a packer, putting things on the shelves. That was some time ago in Kentish Town, in north London, and that was the only one that I could remember. So, the thing was a dream to see coloured people in those positive situations. I feel so great to see how things have progressed by leaps and bounds.

* *Partner or 'Pardner'– informal savings clubs, where individuals in a group would save a weekly amount for a set time and one member of the group would draw the full amount. They would begin again and rotate until everyone in the group had drawn. This scheme was widely used by many*

people to buy houses, send for relatives, start businesses, etc. This activity is called 'Sou-sou hand' in some islands.

Credit unions are a more formalised savings and loan clubs with a strong tradition in the Caribbean, and many people coming to England during this period benefited from such schemes and continued the tradition upon arrival.

Hornsey Credit Union, in north London, was one of the first and most prolific of these credit unions. Set up as a co-operative in the early sixties, it produced The Hornsey Rules for the governance of credit unions.

CECIL WILSON

*Born in 1917, Mr Wilson had lived and worked
in Panama and the United States before moving
to England in the 1950s.*

I came to England in 1956 when I was 39 years old. I came up by boat and travelled alone, although I did get a girlfriend on that boat. Her name? Lord, O! The name bothers me now – I don't remember her name but it was a nice young lady. We travelled together and were friends until I got off the boat.

When we got off, she was going to Stoke Newington, in east London, while I was going to Clapton, in the same area. So, every night I would go up to her apartment and I went back to my place in the morning. This went on until I sent for my proper girlfriend in Jamaica who would later become my wife.

I did have a friend called Lascelles who prepared that room for me, and it was he who received me when I came up to England. I also had a cousin who used to wash and cook for me when I first arrived.

Well, the first job I got was as a carpenter at J&W Bundocks in Clapton. That was my first job in this country. I stayed in the carpentry trade and then left it because of the cold weather. I was working outside and after I left that job I went to a factory, J G Ingrams & Son in Hackney Wick, making hot water bottles and such like. I got out of the cold and got settled in at this factory.

I was there until I sent for my girlfriend — my right girlfriend (who was in Jamaica), not the one I was with here. This one, the one who had been on the boat with me, had a baby boy for me, but since I arranged to send for my girlfriend, I decided not to keep in touch with her anymore. Apparently, she got married after I left her, before my future wife got here. Right now, if she and that baby — he's a man now, of course — but if he and I were to knock together shoulder to shoulder, I wouldn't know him. He never grew up with me and I don't know anything about how he turned out.

Anyway, I never liked boys, I love girl children. It's funny for me to say so but it's true. I have another son back home and he must be in his 50s now because he was born in 1943. My first daughter, (which is not my wife's child; she was born long before I got married), was also born in 1943, the same year as the boy but to a different woman. At that time I was in Panama, doing auxiliary work in a hospital.

After a time in Panama I returned to Jamaica and then travelled to America, where I worked in a gunpowder factory. This was during the war. I went to the States as a volunteer from Jamaica.

The job was so dangerous that when you reached the door to enter the building you had to take off your shoes because they could have ignited the powder and cause an explosion. That powder was a dangerous thing, for sometimes you would be working on the machine in there and you alone would be operating equipment in one room because it was so sensitive. As soon as that powder goes inside that machine it can cause a fire to break out, but, if that happened, all you had to do was use one of the two escape doors — and run for your life.

Only thing: don't use the one in front because if that machine was rolling in this particular direction and you ran to the front door, the impact from the machine could blow you down. You were better off taking the door at the side and running out the building. As I said, it was very dangerous work. That was back in 1944.

Before that, when I was in Panama, I'd heard about them taking men to America. The first time it was for farm work but I didn't want to do that, I wanted to work inside, so later I went to the factory making gunpowder, gunshot and all that jazz.

In 1949, the fare to England was £28, but when I came here I paid £75. The reason I came is that I had a friend back home called Reggie Pennant and he was working at the movie theatre at a place called Crossroads, in Kingston, Jamaica, and he happened to lose that job. But, the problem was that he had just married and his wife had a little baby who wasn't even a year old yet when he lost the job in 1948.

He came to me and said: "Cecil, you're a carpenter by trade and I haven't got no trade. I lost the job I had so Saturday coming I don't know what I'm going to give the wife for housekeeping."

He told me that there was a boat in the harbour, *The Jamaica Producer*, and we should make the both of us stowaway and go to England. At the time I already had my passport but I said "No". The fare was only £28, I wasn't going to stow away. So, I went to another friend named Aubrey Wilson, who was no relation to me, and he said "Yes", but as the time got closer and they were just getting ready to set off, Aubrey changed his mind.

As the boat was ready to pull up anchor, Aubrey jumped off but Reggie did travel and when they reached a certain point he came out of hiding and made friends with some of the workers and got himself some work on the boat and landed in England safe and sound. He didn't suffer any penalty at all.

He settled in London and got a job and everything but he never sent a penny home to his wife, Sybil. I can well remember I used to have a little shop in Maxwell Avenue, and I recall that Reggie's wife was hard up and needed money to pay the rent and she came to me with Reggie's old bicycle and asked me to hold on to it – that is to say give her some money for it to pay the rent, which I did.

At that time she was a lovely Indian girl, you know, and it went on and went on – and I did want to get with her but she wouldn't yield – but anyway, she managed to get some money to retrieve the bicycle and I gave it back to her. I did gain her in the end and she came and helped me in the shop because I didn't have any assistance at that time.

Then one Monday morning in December 1949, I left her alone in the shop while I went to buy goods in town and when I came back the shop was locked up, so I went to the back and asked the neighbour what happened to Sybil and she told me that she'd got a telegram telling her to get ready to go on a boat that was coming into harbour, so she'd locked the shop and gone to get her passport and pack her suitcase.

What happened is that it wasn't Reggie exactly who wrote to her but he was instrumental in that someone he knew had seen her picture and liked the look of this nice Indian girl, so he wrote to invite her to England and she went in December 1949.

When I came here in 1956, it was she who arranged a salesman to provide some winter clothes and a paraffin lamp for me. She was living with Reggie then, but he was a stay-away boy; he would never stay one place. Sometimes he would go and leave her for weeks. It so happened that after some time away he left permanently and they divorced. He then went and lived with a white woman until he died from cancer.

Now, I had come to England as a general traveller. As I said, I had been to other places, I even lived in Holland for some years, but I was so curious to know what England was like. In the end I had a good friend called Lammy who was from Jamaica. He persuaded me to come to England and got the room for me at Clapton, near Homerton Hospital.

When my girlfriend came here 11 months after me, the landlord where I was living said no women allowed, so I got a room off Mare Street in Hackney, near the town hall, and when my Missis came here that's where we slept for the first night. We lived there just over a year and this fellow bought a house and we rented a big room from him.

At that time I was working at J G Ingrams & Son doing carpentry work. Now, there was an Irish fellow there and he wanted my job, right, so him do all kinds of things trying to make things go wrong so he could get that job. And, once, something went wrong with a batch of materials and they took me off that job and put him on it.

All right, I didn't do one thing except one day I was going on the tube and saw a notice up: "Station man wanted", so I took down the address and I wrote to them at London Transport and they sent and called me and I went for the interview and got the job. That's how I went to work on the underground (train).

I was on the underground for a year and nine months and then the bus was paying more so I asked for a transfer to go and work on the buses. In all, I worked with the Transport from 1969 till 1982.

After that I went to live in America for two years,

came back here for a few months and then went to live in Holland for another two years and came back to England in 1985.

Do you know, from I came here in '56 till now I haven't been back to Jamaica? I don't know how come but I never went back there. I never wanted to go. I leave my mother and father in Jamaica. I am the only child that they had, I have neither brother nor sister.

Now, when I came here, I came here for five years. I started to save and to send money home, and by 1973 I did have money home and so I wrote to the building society out there to see if I could try and get a house and they wrote and told me, yes, when I was ready.

At that time £10,000 could buy a house. So I wrote to my mother and she wrote back to me and never gave me a word of encouragement at all. She wrote that the Jamaica that I left behind was not the same place any more. I still insisted that I wanted to buy a house there and I wrote back to her and told her the same thing and she wrote and told me, "Look, if you're fed up of England, you have a lot of family in America, so try Eric or Etta, your cousins to let them help you get through there."

Those were the instructions from my mother, who never gave me any encouragement to go back home. All the money that I sent out there, it's still out there now and that money won't be inherited by me. I'm not going out there to use it. If any of my daughters wants to go out there and inherit it, that's up to them. As for me, I have no intention of ever going there at all. If none of the children wants to inherit their legacy then the government will step in and seize all of it.

I tell you what, my mother had 20 brothers and sisters. Her mother had 17 kids and her father had three more outside the marriage, making 20 of them. Out of those 20 not one is alive today. My mother was the last out of those 20 and she herself is now dead. So, I have neither auntie nor uncle out there. Cousins and so on, yes, but no other relations and I don't have any intention to go back to the country of my birth.

You have to realise that just about everybody who came here from Jamaica came for five years, you know; said let them earn money and go back home. In my case it will soon be nine fives since I came, right? But all the discouragement came from my mother so you could say that my mind is now poisoned towards Jamaica.

When I came here the Prime Minister was Anthony Eden, a conservative. I would say that time goes by and none the worse, because during my working days I never knew what it was go to up to the Labour Exchange to go and get a penny in welfare benefits, and I continued working all my working days until I retired; I was never out of a job.

I left the carpentry work from 1969 and then went to the underground and after that on the buses until I finished working and retired. And I never experienced any prejudice none at all from I came to this country. I was here from 1956 and I got help from Jews. A Jew got a flat for me and I was there until I moved to another place which another Jew helped me to get.

It looks so funny now because, remember my wife and I met in 1951 and lived together until I came to England and then sent for her. Well, the funny part about it is that we lived together and never used any protection (contraception) at all. It wasn't to say we didn't want a baby until we were married or anything like that – it just worked out that way and then she came here we got married on the 14 March 1959. Then, in 1961, we had our first daughter, in 1963: second daughter, 1965: third daughter, 1967: the fourth child – another daughter.

See how funny it looks, because as I said, we had lived together in Jamaica, came here and lived together for three years practically and she never produced a baby until after we were married and there was no "fix" or protection, whatsoever. You see how life works out?

Our first house, at Stamford Hill in north London was just to rent, not to buy, and we lived there from 1963. The house was empty and I had to draw some money from the bank to furnish and decorate it and when I worked out how much I had spent on that house I decided to look for a house to buy. I found one off Seven Sisters Road, in Tottenham, north London, which cost £2,800. That was in 1963, and that was where the third girl was born, right in that house.

Now, after all these years of going to visit America, well, I'm going there to settle. What made me decide to leave England for good? Well, the rest of my family is there and I wouldn't mind staying here but you see it's like this: during the day I am at my club and when I leave there to go home and when I close that door behind me, there's not a god soul to talk to; so that's what I take to heart.

When I went to America last year my daughter said to me, "Daddy, you alone live in England, why not change your mind and come to America to live?" So, we went to the embassy same time and we got the papers sorted out. So, that's where we are now; I'm ready to leave. And when I go I know I will have all the company on earth, because I have so many grandchildren.

The younger generation coming up now in England, I don't know how they will exist. From I came here I never had an idle day but these ones coming up now, what are they going to do? Some of them are not working; there's no work for them. How are they going to exist? How are they going to buy a house? It's too hard for them now. I don't know how they will pull through.

Soon after this interview, Mr Wilson went to live in the United States.

DOREEN PHILLIPS

*Arrived in England from Guyana, South America,
in December 1963.*

It wasn't my desire to come to London, where they called it the "Mother Country". I never wanted to come. My experiences in Guyana, under British rule in the colonial days, is that we had a lot of English people, so we knew that there were prejudices then with the whites, because they had the best houses, the best jobs and everything.

My husband came first and he decided to bring us over. I never liked it from the beginning; never liked it before I arrived here anyway, so that made matters worse. I found fault with everything.

I brought two children with me (my husband had brought the eldest). When we landed here, all I know is that it was extremely dark and dismal for day-time, since I was accustomed to the sunshine. But, I remember I had my son in my arm and another one tugging along, and I was trying to get my suitcase.

I was wearing a suit, high-heeled shoes, and a hat. In those days, you would think, oh, you're going to this place and you wanted to be well-dressed. All I know is that my hat was on one side. I don't know which side it was going. The shoe heel must have dropped off because I think I was walking with the shoe on upside down. And my son had wet me through and through so my suit was soaked right through to the back and I was dying to get out of it. Anybody looking at me would think I'd wet myself because we had those terry nappies and on the plane they didn't have many facilities for the children. So, for me, landing at Heathrow airport was a complete disaster.

And, when I got to where I was supposed to be staying, I stood in the middle of this room my husband had rented and looked around. I said, "Is this it?" That was all. After that, I had to get used to it. I sort of plunged right into things because my husband was working and I had no time to sit and cry. I had to get up and get my kids sorted out with coats and such.

He said, "You know something? This is a hard country, you've got to think."

He gave me five pounds to do the shopping. I had to put money in the gas, I had to put money aside for light; everything. And, I remember it was the 18th December, a few days before Christmas. He told me there was a shop called Anthony Jackson, which is now Tesco's, and I had to go there to do the shopping. And to get from one place to the next you had to go on this underground tube train.

I used to stand at the top of the escalator looking down and asking myself, "do I have to go down that?" But, I had no choice. I asked somebody to help me, which they did and I went down and did the shopping. But, I remember shopping with that five pounds my husband gave me and I bought everything I needed.

He'd said to me, "Make sure you leave money back to pay for my fares to work." Honest. And it worked. I even bought a bottle of wine for Christmas. Our Christmas meal was chicken and a bottle of wine, and we had all the fancy bits.

But, I had to put money aside for the coats each week, because we took some coats from the salesman. We couldn't go to the shop (and just buy outright), so the salesman came: these Jewish people. They would bring blankets, coats and whatever, woollies, bedspreads, and you paid something each week. Then, I gave my husband the rest for his fare, three pence – three old pence – bus fare. Five pounds lasted you all week.

I used to try and pinch and save to send money home. Even a pound was a lot of money back home in those days and although we could hardly afford it, I had to try and help out. But, while his mum and his family were here, mine were there and I wasn't working so it meant taking something out of what he was giving me, and I had to hide to do this and he must have suspected. One day he found all the stubs for the postal orders, so that's why I had to go and get a job.

Initially, settling in was hard, but you soon got used to it. When I had to go to register for the doctor, the dentist, whatever, I had to get this insurance number, but they were very helpful. Whether because at that time there was an influx of immigrants coming into the country (and they did ask for people to do jobs on the buses and the public transport: the jobs that the white people weren't doing), so as long as you were prepared to do the menial jobs you had no problems.

Going for your benefits or whatever they used to give in those days wasn't a problem, from my experience. You got your registration, you got your family allowances, you got help, you had social workers coming to the home to see if you were

OK, if you were settled in and they used to see the children settled at school.

During those times they used to take a lot more interest in the children to see they had milk and cod liver oil. I couldn't work because of three small children, but I got a bit bored and it was a case where you lived in one room and you shared the facilities. Fortunately for me, I shared with people that I knew; friends, and we cleaned and looked after the place well and the landlord for the building was so pleased with the way we ran the place that he eventually bought another house and he gave us the whole place to live in.

So, we were running the house and keeping the place clean, paying him rent and so on. Then, it was easy to pick up a job, you could have walked out from one and go into another; factory jobs, menial jobs. I decided to look for a job and a friend came to me and she said, "Look, I just got a job in this factory and they're doing evenings, so if you want an evening job I'll look after your children."

So, we did it that way and I started doing the job in this factory and when I worked in that factory I could see the segregation. The blacks were on one side, the whites were on one side. We sort of got all the worst bits to do, the sweeping up and such things. We were packing sweets and they were packing sweets; handling the things, but the blacks were doing all the dirty jobs. Then they would use remarks like, "What's smelling like that?", you know? Them sort of things because they used to say that black people stink.

I'm very hot-tempered so when I heard that I'd say, "What the hell's going on here?", speaking to the others, but they were so desperate for their jobs that they didn't respond. I didn't care, 'cause I didn't want to stay. I would have done anything to come out of the country.

Anyway, one of the days when they were carrying on

with their nonsense the supervisor for the factory was having an inspection day. And she was walking through the factory and she looked over and straight away that woman picked up the division. I'll never forget that day. She stood there and she looked at us and she came straight over and asked everybody in my group, "Are you happy in your work?"

They all said, "Yes, ma'am."

I said, "No, I'm not happy."

And she said, "Do you want to talk about it?"

So, she told me to leave what I was doing and she took me up to her office and I told her exactly what was happening. That woman had travelled and, apparently, she mixed with all sorts of people and that is why she picked up the tension straightaway.

We started to talk and she asked me if I'd like to move from there; work on the machines or do something different? I said, "Anything away from there", and by the next day when I came in I was moved. I pushed myself out of that situation. I worked with those people as the only black in the section I moved to for ten years, doing that part-time job and then I had my daughter. I never had a day's prejudice from them any more. But, my own people? They were upset and said, "Why did she get that thing?" But they didn't want to speak up for themselves.

When my daughter was old enough I came out to go and do the job which I had really wanted to do, which was clerical work. And that is where the prejudice is today. In those days it wasn't too bad. You had the blacks fighting against the whites, you had the Teddy Boys and this and that. Back then, you could have seen it; you knew who were your enemies (although you were working right alongside them), but this time it is worse because you can't see it.

I worked for twenty five years in the clerical job that I took early retirement from in 1998. That is where I really saw the people as they were and I took it up with them. I even had the industrial tribunal involved because they wouldn't give you promotion if you were black; they would keep you on one job and they would give you bad reports.

So, you can't make that comparison with the '50s and '60s with what's going on today. It's today they've got prejudice. Don't worry about going in the churches and ting, the people weren't used to black people. You were in a church and a whole influx of black people come in, how d'you expect them to react? You know they're scared, it's not that they don't want you. Rather, they're not used to you.

People would say, "Oh, that's years ago, those things don't happen now", but it's happening today. I've got my children in jobs and they tell me what's happening, things you wouldn't expect. My daughter was born here, and at work they put people over her, so what do you call that?

You see, they're more wise out there; they know how to squeeze you. Back then, back in the '50s and '60s, it was just blatant prejudice. Today, they're not going to tell you you're black, but they're going to do everything to make it hard for you. And this is where the prejudice is, this is what we've all got to work on today. But I had some very happy days in the 1960s because we lived as a community.

There was more community spirit; we looked out for each other. Nobody goes and sees each other if they're sick today. That didn't use to happen in the '60s, so those weren't the bad old days.

Today, these are the bad days. You can sick and die and you don't hear from anybody, but we used to visit each other's homes, you didn't need appointments; you walked in. You're in one room, you sit together around the paraffin heater, you put the kettle on the paraffin heater, you made tea.

You keep my children, I keep yours. Could I ask my neighbour today, "Keep my children, I'm going to work in the evening" if I don't pay a hundred pounds? I did that in the '60s, so which are the best days? I mean, tell me. We used to arrange to pick up each other's children from school. You pick up mine today, I pick up yours tomorrow, although we didn't have much money, so which are the best days?

We partied till morning, police weren't bothering you. I come to you, you keep a party in your room. You charge two shillings to go in. A friend kept a party in her room and I said to my friends, "We're not going there early, you know, let's go late." Because the place was so small, it used to be ram-jam. So, what we did was we'd go there about 12 o'clock in the night and when she saw us lot coming she'd say to those in the party, "You lot have been in here a long time, come out so the new lot can come in." So, we'd go in and stay until in the morning.

We went to basement parties, the pubs and there were local things, and you didn't have all these airs and graces. When I came to this country, the first place I was introduced to was a pub and I said, "No, we don't go in them places in Guyana."
They said, "What's the matter with you? Come on, this is London. You drink in here." So, we used to go in the pub. We used to drink Guinness or VP Wine. Who didn't drink didn't go to the pub. Our fun was: we finished work Friday and we'd go to the pub for a drink.

Every Saturday night there was a house party. We hadn't a lot of money, so the fun was the Saturday blues or the pub. And, if you could get a babysitter, you were in the pub with your friends. You ain't got to worry yourself. You would leave your children home, who's downstairs can keep an eye on them.

Music-wise, my favourite boy was John Holt. I loved a lot of Ray Charles, the old songs, and Nat Cole. But then

I would get away with the odd reggae-type thing: what they used to call Blue Beat. I had a good time. I'm not saying that I'm not having a good time now, but I miss the closeness that we black people had. Now, we don't have it.

You had your prejudice between your own blacks, 'cause you'd be telling me you come from this island and my island's bigger than your island, this nonsense. We had all that. But it used to be fun to get to know somebody that came from another island 'cause you learned about their culture, their ways.

One of my best friends was from Jamaica and we lived next door. Because we talked all the time over the fence, her husband decided to cut out a piece of the fence so that I could go in to see her and she could come over to me. And she would say, "What you cooking today?"

She made me eat this ackee* dish and then I used to make bread and pass it over to her. This went on so till the husband would come in and used to shout, "What, no bread ain't coming over today?" That's how we used to live. We don't do that now. It's everybody for themselves and it's becoming a narrow and selfish world.

I think if we had unity between black people, regardless of where we come from, we would fight the prejudices. It's like, if you got any protest going on out there, you see how many black people go out there. It's mostly whites holding up the banner for something that concerns me; there's no unity with us. As soon as anybody does speak up, others don't want to say anything, they just stay in the corner. If I decide to open my mouth, they'll say, "She mouth too big", although you're talking up for them, and then when you're looking round behind you, they're gone and it's you alone fighting the faceless monster. I know for sure that the Jamaicans made it a bit easier for the black people here by speaking up.

In employment, we've done the menial jobs that

needed to be done, like running the transports, which was essential to this country because the English man ain't coming out of his house on a Sunday. He don't want to work, but they're doing it now because times are hard.

The cleaning jobs, the nursing, in the health services, black people have contributed more. They went into it, although the money was never enough. The people that run the transport system, the cleaners, the people that keep the places clean, and things like that, they're the ways that black people have contributed a lot in this country.

* *Jamaica's national dish: ackee paired with saltfish (salted cod).*

GLORIA BROWNE

Came to England from Jamaica at the age of 16. After a career as an entertainer and as a store detective, she worked with her husband in his estate agency.

My mother had been here for about three years before she sent for me. Unfortunately, the departure from Jamaica wasn't smooth. I am not a good traveller and even when I was in school I used to be sick travelling on trains, buses and cars. That is why my mother put me on the plane because I could not take the boat, but I was still very sick coming on the plane as there was a lot of turbulence.

We stopped in Newfoundland and that was the first time that I saw snow. I did not have any warm clothes, so the hostess gave us all blankets to wrap up to go into this big aircraft shelter to have breakfast, but I could't eat anything because I was so sick; vomiting and all that.

When I got to Heathrow my mother wasn't there to meet me and they put us on a bus to Victoria. But,

the biggest shock for me was coming into London itself, you could hardly see anything. It was April and
the weather was so bad that all I could see was a little dim street light and the nearer you came into London all you could see were chimneys and black smoke
and I could not believe they were houses on top of
one another. They looked like buildings and factories.
That's all I could see. I'd never seen anything like that.

Before we came here, like most people that I have spoken to, I thought England was a golden city, a golden
country; the Mother Country. One of the beliefs was that
London's streets were paved with gold, but because my
aunt, my mother and cousin were here before, they had
sent to tell me what it was like but it still did not sink in
until I got here and then it was a shock.

After settling in, I started evening classes, but I soon
got bored with it because they were teaching what I had
gone through in ABC class back home. I just continued
with shorthand, which, I'm afraid to say I did not finish
either, but I did get a job very quickly as a junior clerk in
an office doing filing. I think I was paid £1.75 a week. It
was a little bit of money.

Remember the old shilling was twelve old pence, so a
shilling was twenty five pence. You could go to the shop
or the market and ask for two pence worth of this or
sixpence worth of that, so you could buy a lot of things
and prices were not very high.

One problem, though, is that all you could get was black
or white pepper, there were no spices. If they smelled
your cooking they always passed remarks that you were
cooking dog food. Their food was just greens: cabbage
they boiled in water and had with potatoes and sausages,
or a bit of ham. They weren't used to chicken or meat;
they would only have that at Christmas or at Easter.

One woman in the office and I began to be very close
friends. She went away on holiday and when she came

back she said, "I meant to send you a postcard but I didn't know your last name. She asked me what it was and I said, "Harrison" (my maiden name), and she said, "What? that's an English name. Where did you get it from?"

And I said, "You people do not know your history or geography at all. You know that the Caribbean or the West Indies were ruled by the British people, therefore they took our heritage and gave us their names, so I have an English name: Harrison, and we live in houses."

They thought we lived in tree houses and that we came from Africa. I showed her some photos of where I came from and she said, "You came from places like this, and you come to this country and you come to a place like this?" And she was so shocked.

They were really backward; they did not know anything. In school back home we learned about England and, although I was a child, we had to learn geography and subjects like that.

I happened to have an argument with one of the girls and she came out with, "Oh, I wish you could speak proper English." So, one of the other girls said to her, "Oh, Sylvia, you know that these people speak better English than we do."

I did not have much trouble getting a job in an office then. A lot of people went and got jobs in the factories but I found it quite straight forward getting the office work, although the factory work paid a bit more. I had just left school and I did not have any real qualifications, so that was one of my first jobs.

One thing: the factory paid you five pounds or six pounds, something like that, and out of that money people had to buy their food, pay their fares, and a lot of them saved money to send home for their family. That's how my mother managed to send for me to come over here.

You know, it was a hard time but I was lucky because

the house I came to where my aunt and mum were living belonged to a friend of the family. It was one of the larger Victorian-type houses, and it was quite comfortable. We had to share the kitchen with other tenants but it was quite reasonable. I am pleased to say I did not have problems going about knocking on doors trying to rent somewhere and being turned away.

Nearly two years after I came here, my mother had to go home to Jamaica. At that time I had fallen in love with a young man when I was seventeen, and Mama said it would be good if I got married before she left. Well, I did get married and got pregnant more or less straightaway and had one boy in 1957 and one in 1958, and one more just as we were going into 1960. So, I had three sons while still in my teens and that was a big responsibility, I'm telling you.

Well, the marriage didn't work. I went into it naïve but very soon I became wise. There and then I was on my own bringing up three babies. Other relatives here helped me along and, luckily, I had a very good doctor who gave me advice about where to get help, because I had so much depression and worries. But, being the type of person I am I couldn't be contented with life just as it was, so I tried to help myself.

I knew some people who were in show-business so I decided to have a go. While the children were still small I did get involved in the industry and made a few records. At that time it was Ska and Blue Beat that was in. I was known as "Little Gloria" and sang with a friend of mine called Clive, so we were Clive and Little Gloria.

One of the most popular tunes we had was called *Money, Money, Money* on the Blue Beat record label. It goes, "Money, money, money, money, money — that's all you want; you want money!"

We had our pictures in the music magazines and, by

talking to other people in the showbiz circle I also got into belly dancing and was known as Princess Fatima.

I remember the first job I got was when the agency sent me up north to this working men's club but I was not very successful because I was too inhibited. They didn't like me at all.

One time, there were agents who brought over these dancers from Sierra Leone who were touring England and when they left, other agents wanted to form their own topless dance group with coloured girls and they approached me but I said, "Oh, no, I'm the mother of three little boys. I'm not going out there to do that." They said, "Oh, don't be daft!", and they offered to send me overseas but I still said no.

They didn't like it because they said, "Why are you in this business? You don't drink, you don't smoke, you don't go to orgies." So I was not in the business very long. I had to come out as I couldn't take all what was going on in the show-business world, but I did enjoy the singing, the dancing and all the travelling.

Entertainment back in those days was mainly the house parties. Either we would visit friends or they would visit us and we would have the radiogram. And you always had a selection of blues records or we would go to the cinema to see stars like Elizabeth Taylor or Jane Mansfield, or else we went on outings regularly.

Well, after that I wasn't actually working, I was just looking after the children and getting government help with that. It wasn't much, just a few pounds a week, so I went back to work and got a job in a factory where they made electric lamps. I stayed there for about three years and then I left and got a job as a cashier-clerk in a furniture store and I was with them for about five years, and while I was there I took a course.

At that time, computers and telex were just coming in,

so I took a course in telex operating but after I did that I could not get a job. I would have had to have about a year's experience, so I stayed in the job as a cashier-clerk, and then I went to do security as a store detective. I was given a company car and I travelled all over England and I think I've been into every court house in England to prosecute people for shoplifting and cashiers for pocketing the takings.

I was very good at my job but it was hard to have to prosecute them especially when they started to cry. Some even got down on the floor and started kissing my feet. And one or two you used to feel sorry for, but then there were other ones who used to say, "Is this what you leave your country and come here to do: to spy on white people and treat us like thieves?"

It was not for me to let them off, all I had to do was take them to the manager's office and he would take it from there: call the police and so on.

When I became a born-again Christian, I started to let them off. I would go up to them and tell them not to do it. Before, I had this long record of arrests and it started falling, so my bosses started to enquire why it was falling. I tried to make excuses, but, eventually, they sent a supervisor from another head office to question me. I had to tell him the truth and then I said, "Sorry, I can't do this job any more."

They gave me some time to think it over, but one day I caught a woman shoplifting and she was crying and telling me how life was hard and that she couldn't manage and I had to witness to her about how God can provide for her and the manager came out of his office and heard me talking to the woman and he told me to leave my god at home when I come to work. I told him I couldn't do that and he said if I carried on I would get the sack, so I resigned.

I needed the money and I had my children to think

about but it's like the Lord spoke to me and said, "For all these years you have been praying and saying , 'Lord, if I am not supposed to be doing this job, release me', and now here is your chance."

I know that God promises to provide for us, so I just smiled and resigned. The company gave me a month to think about it in case I wanted to change my mind, but I knew another job would open up for me.

My husband was in business and, after a time, I decided I didn't want to stay at home and be a full-time mother, so I suggested working with him in the business. At first, he didn't want me to but then he agreed and from then that is what I have been doing.

The Lord has been providing wonderfully.

SUSAN RICKETTS

Retired x-ray technician, aged 75. She came from Jamaica in July 1956. Before leaving the island, she worked for a company manufacturing detergents, run by an English manager. He told her he couldn't understand why she wanted to leave her lovely country to go to England, where he was from and had no intentions of returning to.

When I came I lived in Aldgate, east London, at first, but it was such a small place, only one room with six other people. I couldn't stand it — every day I had tears in my eyes.

There was an outside toilet, freezing weather and we had to use a bucket to wash ourselves. I wasn't used to any of this; it was terrible. In Jamaica, we were used to space and clean conditions. However, things got better and we were able to move.

If my experience of London was as terrible as some people had it, I would have gone back home a long time ago. I heard about how some people suffered with trying to find housing or jobs and such like, although I didn't have those awful experiences. But, after living in those terrible conditions in Aldgate, we went to live in Tottenham, north London, to a house owned by some black people.

It was clean, tidy and had more space than we had before and we had the use of a bathroom at last. Most people had to go and use the public baths in those days, which was something that I never had to do. The thought of it just put me right off, so, back in Aldgate, I had bought myself a bucket which I kept especially for myself to wash in. We stayed at the house in Tottenham, which we rented, until we were able to buy our own house in the same road.

Before I came to this country, I had had a good job in Jamaica working for a company which produced soap, oil, perfumes and that sort of thing, and the manager was so nice to me that he begged me not to go to England. He told me that he came from there and there was no way he was going back, so he tried to put me off, but I really wanted to go and see for myself and, besides, my husband was there, so I was going to join him.

The manager told me that if I went and didn't like it, he would pay for me to come back and he would give me back my job. That never happened, though, because I was determined to go to England and work. Even though things might have been bad to start with, I wanted to see it through. I couldn't really go back to Jamaica and tell them that I had failed.

My motto is, "Don't worry over anything." I'm nearly 76 and my attitude to life is not to fret and worry about things but to be grateful for what I have. Every day I get up and thank God for another day.

When I first came, I worked with a Jewish woman at a

dressmaking factory. The place was so dusty that I couldn't stand it. I was earning £4.12.6 a week and out of that we always used to send money home (to Jamaica).

I had a friend who worked as a technician at the old German Hospital (now closed) in east London and she got me introduced there. I had my training in the x-ray department and worked there until the hospital closed down. After that, I went to work at another hospital before going on to work at North Middlesex Hospital for 18 years before I retired.

At first my ambition was to go into nursing but, in those days, nurses had to live in and my husband wouldn't put up with that, so I had to give up the idea of becoming a nurse. But, I did enjoy the work I did in the lab and I found I got on quite well with my co-workers.

There was one time, though, that I was getting a lot of stick from one Irish girl. She decided to pick on me and tell me to go back where I came from. One of the other workers, another Irish girl, told me that the next time she told me that I should go back where I came from I should tell her that the reason she wouldn't go back where she came from was because they had to burn newspaper (as fuel) to boil potatoes to cook and eat. But, I could stand up for myself and after a while she stopped bothering me because, although she could dish it, she couldn't take it when I answered her back. She even tried to get me into trouble by telling the manager that I wasn't doing my work properly but the manager told them all that she was quite satisfied with my work.

I always remember mixing with different races of people from my childhood and that followed right through to when I came here. I was also taught to hold my head up and to try my best in all things. My father was in the army and, although we might have been poor, we were never dirty. If we had two pieces of clothes, one would be on your back whilst the other was washed and put up. We learned to help ourselves from a very early age and there was always discipline.

Since retiring, I do a lot of charity work for organisations like Age Concern, Victim Support, Haringey Disabled Consortium, the Community Health Council, plus Imperial Cancer Research Fund, and I work for the church. I have given up some of the community work since retiring as it was all getting too much. I'm not as young as I used to be.

As to the church, when I first came here, I went to the Anglican (since that was what I was used to from home) but after three weeks no one spoke to me at all, not even the priest; they were so cold and unfriendly, so I tried going to another church: same thing. I tried the Baptists: they were no better, so I went back to the first church and decided that's where I was going to stay, whether they liked it or not.

After some time a few people began to say, "Hello", and even the priest started to mumble a few words. More blacks started to come and, today, we have more blacks there than whites, and it's much friendlier and nicer than in the old days.

I heard about a lady who went to a church back in the sixties and everybody ignored her. She was the only black but she was determined to stay and to become part of the fellowship, so she went to a meeting and offered to help out with the church maintenance. Well, they told her to clean the floors and the toilets and showed her a bucket and brush. She got down on her hands and knees and cleaned the whole place. It was so bad that it was like the place hadn't been cleaned in years, but she took her time and did it. They must have been laughing at her, she didn't care.

All I can say is that would not have been me; no way. Get down on my knees! After I never used to clean floors in Jamaica, why should I come here and do that? They must be mad! But we did go through some trials with the churches, of all places, over here in the sixties. Nowadays, if black people don't go to them, the chuches would be almost empty.

I love to travel. I have been to Zimbabwe, New York, Amsterdam, to Israel several times and many other places around the world, but I don't think I would live anywhere but in England because my family is here. Also, I have spent so many years in this country working and giving to the system. The time has now come for me to get my dues.

EDRICK LAWMAN

*Businessman and community activist who
came to England from Jamaica in 1965. He returned in
the late 1980s, before relocating to Miami, Florida.*

My dad went to live in England in the fifties and I suppose the idea was to work and send for my mother, my brother and I. We all lived with my grandparents and some other cousins. There were quite a few of us in the house, but it didn't feel overcrowded; it felt normal to have all your family around.

So, my dad would write and send us things and when the time came for us to go to England he sent money and they had to get our passports and tickets some time before we actually travelled.

Of course, my brother and I had no idea what was going on for a long time because the grandparents, aunts and uncles did all the arranging like it was some secret undercover operation. We knew that something was happening but we didn't know what exactly.

I remember going to get our photos taken for the passports, which was quite exciting. Looking back at my old passport picture, it looks like a mug shot! It's so funny. There I am staring out like a rabbit caught in the headlights and looking as stiff as a board. It might well have been the first time that my brother and I actually had had our photos taken, so that was a strange new experience.

There was a sense of excitement as the departure date got closer, and by now we were well aware that we were going to "foreign", as they called it. We were like mini celebrities. It felt as though we had hit the jackpot. You could see how much we were either envied, hated or admired — or all three — because we were going to England. The whole school knew about it and the head-master even mentioned it in the morning assembly.

We had our "grips", as we called our little suitcases, and my mum had two red ones while my brother and I each had a small brown case. The day before we left, we had a send off party with nice food like curry goat and ice-cream — not together, of course. And there were people coming to the house to wish us well and give us messages to deliver or to tell us what they wanted us to send them or bring back from that great country "Hinglan".

Well, on the day of departure, we had on our best church clothes with brand new shirts, socks, vests and underpants (the first time we wore vests. After all, we didn't need them in Jamaica). And our shoes were polished and shining like a looking glass. The day before leaving we had gone for our haircuts, so we felt very slick and presentable — or "trash" and "ready", as those rude boys liked to say whenever they were looking good.

When we got to Kingston airport and actually got on the plane I was so excited that I was sure I could hear my heart beating. It was a mixture of anticipation, excitement and fear, but mostly excitement. My brother and I hadn't slept the night before. We kept talking in bed — or rather, whispering — about how the pilot was going to get the "giant bird" to fly up in the air and how he was going to get it back on the ground in one piece. As we were getting on the plane for real that's all I kept thinking about and my heart was thumping like a drum.

Suddenly, when the plane took off and was rushing down the runway I thought my heart was going to beat right out of my chest, but I wasn't the only one who was excited. It turned out that we were not the only ones flying for the first time. Some of the other people started gasping and some were calling for the stewardesses, but that soon got drowned out by the noise of the plane and didn't last for long. I'm sure a few of the older women near us were praying to God.

Once up in the air I felt quesy in my belly, and then when my brother and I looked through the window we saw everything getting smaller and smaller below us. The clouds looked like delicious snow cone (shaved iced) or ice cream.

After a while the pretty stewardesses brought us some nice food to eat and some soda to drink. Those young women were always so beautiful and elegant, and I don't know how they managed to smile so much. I found them mesmerising and told myself that when I grew up I was going to marry one.

We flew for a long time and my brother and I even fell asleep. When we woke up to have some more food it was pitch black outside. Soon after that, the plane landed and we thought we had reached England, but it was just a stop over. I later found out that we'd stopped in Nova Scotia or somewhere like that, perhaps to refuel or pick up more passengers.

One other thing I do remember is that when we came

off that plane it was cold! And I mean cold like my brother and I had never felt in our whole lives. Our teeth were chattering and there was smoke coming out of our noses and mouths, like when you see people smoking cigarettes. We got a kick out that because it made us feel a bit grown up. We got blankets to wrap up in and then we went into a big terminal building for some time and then we were allowed back on to the plane.

We flew for hours — it felt like days since we had left Jamaica. We slept again, woke again, ate again (that was my favourite part of the flight) and then early the next morning we landed at London airport.

My first impression? This was a strange and cold, cold place. It was freezing like when you opened the Frigid-aire, only ten times colder. How could a place be so cold and grey and damp?

And the people around us were all white and pale and they were all dressed in black or grey clothes. I had never seen so many white people before and some of them looked like ones we had seen in books or magazines, except these ones weren't smiling. They looked miserable, angry and busy, rushing here and there.

My dad came to meet us and that was the best thing about being in England at that point. It was good to see him; a friendly face at last. And it was good to see him and Mum together again, although they didn't show a lot of emotion except smiles and hugs. We knew they were just as excited as we were. My dad kept telling my brother and me how much we had grown and how we would be going to school soon.

Outside, there was fog everywhere — that was a new experience for us also — but it looked as if it was clearing up as we drove along. As we were driving we could see so many vehicles on the road with people rushing to and fro.

This was a strange and funny cold country and I'm

wondering how would we live here and when was the sun ever going to come out? Suddenly, I missed my grandparents and my friends, and I wanted to get on the next plane and go back home to Jamaica. I figured I would give it a week or so but after that I didn't want to stay in "Hinglan" any at all.

My dad had a house, which he lived in part of and rented out the rest. It was one of those big Victorian houses in west London. He was a builder and his friends did various different jobs working shifts. They were taking their time to do up the house bit by bit in their spare time when they were not doing their day jobs, and it was in a good enough condition for him to send for us, so here we were.

We lived on the ground floor and there was another family living in the basement. We became good friends with the kids in that family, but the other people living in the house were single working people who were out during the day and back in the evening.

My dad liked it that way because he was a man who believed in people having a purpose in life. He encouraged them to save up for their own place and whenever those single people in the house got married or wanted to send for their kids or family members from abroad he encouraged them to move on and helped them to get a bigger place to rent or to buy.

He became known as a "community man" and he was like that all his life, until my brother and I came to be the same way. We organised community events and providing things like supplementary schools for children who were falling behind in the state schools. All that was later on, of course.

When we came, it took my brother and I a long time to settle and get used to this new place called "home" because all we could think about was how happy and carefree we were in our own country when we used to run and play in the open air, sometimes for miles, hunting birds with our slingshots, going fishing and swimming by the river, pitching marbles and fighting, climbing trees and riding our bicycles. We knew how to wash, cook, clean and iron because our mother and grandmother taught us and made sure we learned those life skills, alongside our other boy and girl cousins.

In comparison to Jamaica, this place was like a prison because there were so many rules about what we couldn't do, where we couldn't go, getting in before dark — and it was always dark so early — four o'clock in the afternoon during the winter in dark, cold England.

Coming from Jamaica was a double-edged sword. On one side, we were seen as "different" and I think some people thought we were backward, while on the other hand most of the other kids admired us and thought we were "exotic" and "foreign". We were expected to know all about the music, style or even the latest swear words coming out of Jamaica.

Jamaicans by nature are not shrinking violets so when it came to running, sports, dancing, singing or any kind of physical activity, we were not backward in coming forward to take part and get noticed. We were also very competitive so that meant my brother and I flew the flag for our little island, even long after we had lost our Jamaican accents and were speaking like the other west London kids in our area.

Well, we did get into fights. We had to because in those days we were picked on because we "talked funny", because we could run fast and win all the races, because we had black skin, because we answered questions and asked a lot of questions in class. You name it, someone always wanted to get us into trouble or mixed up in a dust up. That was until they realised that my brother and I were fearless and we could fight like Muhammad Ali.

Fighting was what we were used to back home, so there was no point anyone forming the fool and thinking they could take us down. If you touched me, you had to touch my brother; and if you touched one of our friends, you had to touch us as well. We didn't go looking for trouble, but we never ran, either, except when it made sense to run and fight another day. It got to the point where we were having to defend other children who were being picked on and racially abused and word soon got round that you didn't mess with "the Jamaicans".

The teachers were just as bad as some of the racialist bullies in those days. They got away with murder and would box you or pinch your ears, or send you outside to go and pick up leaves if they wanted to humiliate you.

I think they were goading us on to fight so they could expel us from the school, but we had been drilled from back home to have respect for our teachers and other people in authority, so we never fell for that. Besides, they were like pussycats compared to the teachers we had in Jamaica, so there was nothing they could do that would break us. They called us nasty words like "wog", "bush babies", "jungle bunnies", "coon", that sort of thing. That was the teachers, you know.

When that happened we learned to bite our lips otherwise we would have been expelled, beaten up or branded "educationally subnormal" and sent to borstal. My brother and I would never give them that satisfaction. Sometimes I bit my lip until it bled just so I wouldn't fall into that trap, but if we had different parents and were not such strong characters, things would have been very different.

It was happening all the time: boys were being sent away for being "too lippy" or "aggressive" or whatever; any excuse. If you didn't know better you would have thought that our black race was alllergic to education the way they carried on.

My mum and dad were very concerned about all the fighting and about us not getting a bad reputation and so they arranged for us to go to better schools outside our area. At first we were upset and confused especially because we didn't want to be separated from our friends, but it turned out to be a good decision because we were able to actually get on with our education.

At first it looked like we were going from the frying pan into the fire because now we were even more in the minority and we still had to put up with a lot of racialism from some of the teachers and students. They were more sneaky and not so directly in your face. But we could prove ourselves using our brains, which they learned to respect us for.

I wanted to say something about church, because my mum was very religious and she insisted that we went to Sunday school. Dad used to go once in a while. He was religious in his own way.

Back home we used to go to the Salvation Army church, but when we came to England there was a big Anglican church near us and Mum decided that was where we should go. So, we went and joined the Sunday school, which was a bit boring so we decided to stay in the main church with her. There weren't many black faces there because I think by the time we arrived word was going around that they were "prejudice" and didn't want to "blacken up" the church. We only heard that later.

As it happened, after a while Mum found a different church not too far away which had a more active Sunday school and a youth club for boys and one for girls, so that was where we settled down. We went to Sunday school on Sunday mornings and on Thursdays we went to the boys' club, where we learned a lot of activities like wood work, playing instruments, sports, and we even went away camping. That was more like what I had been used to in Jamaica, so that was right up my street.

That club really played a big part in shaping our lives and it kept us out of trouble, especially because we got to make friends with people from different races and backgrounds and I'm still in touch with some of those people today.

It was refreshing to have positive places like that club because it was easy to feel very rejected and pressurised in those days. Everywhere you looked you felt that you didn't belong if you were a black person. You were usually expected to do the worse jobs and it was always a case of last in, first out, if they were sacking people.

We were studying in school but there were no great expectations about our future, except from our parents, of course. For them, the sky was the limit and they would always encourage us to think big. You always got that from Jamaican parents. We had ambition imprinted in our brains.

My dad always had the idea that he would start his own business and eventually he did, so that was a big incentive for my brother and I to aim high. Having a dad like ours, we had no choice about keeping on the straight and narrow, and mum was no pushover, either. The word "can't" did not exist in her vocabulary and to this day that is my motivation in life.

After doing my exams, I went to college to study accountancy and business studies. Some of my friends were under pressure to go and get jobs, and some of them got jobs as trainee mechanics or working in factories or whatever. Some couldn't get jobs, but I was fortunate enough to have parents who pushed us to get the most out of our education while we were still young. They used to tell us: "You have your whole life ahead of you. There is a time for everything and girls aren't going anywhere."

Well, that was a good way of pouring cold water on a young man's love life. Besides, most of the good looking girls weren't really interested in studious "professor" types. They wanted guys who had jobs, which meant money, cars and flashy clothes.

I had to find a secret weapon to keep the girls keen without destroying my plans to make something of my life. I definitely wasn't ready to settle down and I most definitely didn't want to be forced to settle down because I had made my girlfriend pregnant. That's how it was in those days, but for me that option was a no-no, so I put most of my energies into different activities rather than courting.

While studying I had a lot of other things on the go, like a part-time job and I belonged to different clubs. I even got to travel and represented my club and my adopted country in sports. Plus, I helped my dad in his business and made some more money that way.

Those opportunities took me out of a limited environment. I enjoyed so many benefits that lots of young men could only have dreamed of. When it came to starting a career, I was ready. I was educated and qualified, so that boosted my confidence.

Small-minded people thought we should never amount to much in life and should stay at the bottom of the pecking order. We had to prove them wrong, and we did.

MARIA DALRYMPLE & NEFERTITI GAYLE

*Maria is a youth worker who came to England as an
eight-year-old. Nefertiti is a performance poet who
came to England when she was four.*

Nefertiti: I came to England in February 1959
on a boat, and I remember the sea was very
blue. I can still see it now: I am leaving Jamaica
and my uncle is giving me some sweets or peanuts
or something like that just as we are about to depart.

And then, walking up the plank to this boat and being packed into a cabin with my mother, brothers and
sister; packed in with all these other people, like on the
slave ships. That's what it reminds me of if we talk about
reflecting back. And I remember being sea-sick and
throwing up. That's it, I remember vomiting after eating
pink ice cream and there was sick all down my new dress.

When we arrived in England it was foggy and I remember my mother pointing to my father and saying,
"There's your dad", and him standing on the dockside

waving.

It was so cold and misty and there was no colour; it was colourless, unlike where we had just come from, and I just thought, "What is this place?"

I just remember we were couped-up in a house at Somerleyton Road in Brixton, near a club called Allardyce Club, where, much later, Lynton Kwesi Johnson would play the sound systems. We were in a typical room with other Caribbean people and we had a bunk bed where we children used to sleep, and my mother and father used to sleep in the double bed.

My mother had a child every year, so I was six, my brother was five, another brother was four and my sister was two. The place was so claustrophobic and my father used to go with other women. He had a woman in the house so he would go off and that led to him quarrelling with my mother. That was something that stood out in my mind.

Once, I saw him hit my mother and then push her outside the door and them taking me inside to comfort me because I was crying. That experience was traumatising for a child and I think it affected the way I thought about men later on in my life.

Maria: I came here in 1963, when I was nine. I came on my own but my parents paid for me to be escorted on the BOAC (British Overseas Airways Corporation) plane.

There I was with my little BOAC badge and my little pink accordion pleated dress, pink cardigan, bobby socks, white shoes and, of course, my hat.

My grandmother, my father's mother, organised every thing: getting my clothes made and so on. Parting was quite hard. I left the house of my mother's mother, Mother Dear, as we called my grandmother, and a car took me to my other grandmother, Mother Lara, my father's mother, and I promised that I would never forget them and that I would write.

Yes, there were tears but it was an adventure; you were going to England to meet people who had sent you Christmas boxes and birthday presents. I must have been about five when I had last seen my dad and about six when my mum left Jamaica to join him. So, now, we were going to be reunited, and that was exciting.

The plane stopped in New York and we were taken off and put in an office where this teleprinter spewed out paper. Then they gave us something to eat and we got back on the plane. That was all I saw of New York.

Then, when we came to England, I remember being in a car surrounded by my dad wearing a woolly coat, someone else is driving and we're driving along what I now know to be the Old Kent Road in south London. And it just looks busy but grubby, and I remember these chickens hanging in a butcher's shop, and I'm thinking, "chickens...hanging. Where are the flies? The flies are going to go on them." But, there were no flies and I thought that was strange.

Then, we arrived home: Breakspeare's Road in Brockley, south-east London, which was owned by the Johnson family who were friends of our family, and there was a room at the top which we rented. That house was huge with, what, three stories with a basement and a big garden. When we got home from the airport my mum made me bacon and eggs; that was my first meal in England.

So, now I've got to get used to the food because everything on the journey up to now has been tasteless. And while we're having breakfast I'm repeating messages from Jamaica that I've been told to say: "Miss So and Mr So says to tell you such and such", that sort of thing, and I'm being told by my mum that I'm going to school next week. I'm the eldest child and it's just me and my parents here at this point.

After the meal, I'm given a guided tour of the house and am told where the bathroom is and so on, and there are other families in the house. I'm made welcome by the children who are there, and everybody gets on well with everybody else.

Nefertiti: I had been going to school in Jamaica, which was like a little prep school or nursery school, because I remember writing on a slate with chalk.

My grandmother must have been the one who took me to school. There is a big gap, because my grand-mother was there up to the age of six when I left Jamaica and then I didn't go back there until 1975 and she had died in 1973. So, there is a big hole in my life because I didn't have that contact with her as I'd had as a child. I wish I'd had that contact again and not having had it left a big imprint on me.

There's this mental picture I have of me hanging on to her skirt tail. The most significant thing about leaving Jamaica was leaving my grandmother, and that im-pinged on me as I got older; that everybody had a grand-mother and I didn't have mine around. It still hurts in a way. So, now that I have a grandson I realise the impor-tance of him having a grandmother and of being there for him.

School here was very racist, that's what I remember; it was very, very racist. I was one of the only, if not the only black child there. I don't remember any others around in my year at least. There was one other black girl but she had kind of indian with straight hair. My hair was plaited. And, also, because my mother was, you might as well call her a single parent (although my father came in and out of her life), therefore she didn't have much money and sometimes I went to school with maybe a button missing or something like that. It was difficult. Coming from a working class family you could see that

I was clean but I didn't have much money, so white people used to make fun of me. I was made aware of race at the age of five or six through bullying and also through the teachers who dealt with me. I can't remember any kindness from them. None of them comforted me when I was being bullied and when we played games and had to pair up none of the white kids wanted to pair up with me. But, also, one of the bullies in the school was an older black boy and I used to be frightened of him. He used to pick on anybody and I remember having to run away from him. So, school was awful for me. I was bullied and I was the odd one out and never felt any kindness or love. After a while you forgot about Jamaica as your home and all you think about is the love and kindness of your home with your family where you felt safe from bullying and from being discriminated against.

My mother cooked Caribbean food all the time so it wasn't strange. Her food was things like tripe with broad beans, which, as a child I didn't like but as I got older I liked; and pigtail, and cow foot; everything that was a part of an animal: the foot or the tail, like chicken foot soup, oxtail, that sort of thing. And we always used to get greens, which I didn't like, so I used to stuff them underneath the table. And my mother used to give us a wash out (laxative) with herbs every month, which we hated. But I remember l liked school dinners: chips and mashed potatoes, semolina and tapioca. And I loved sponge and custard, spotted dick and custard, and all of those things.

Maria: I liked school dinners, although I hated custard. Eventually, I got to like apple pie but I could never stand custard, and I remember we used to have to finish our food before we could go up for seconds and I would have to sit there with this custard in front of me which the teacher said I had to eat, but the other kids would scrape it all up and have it so that we could go up for seconds. But, mostly, what I liked about school was the people I met.

My school days were mostly happy. I was happy with the friendships that I made. I got on well with most of the other children. We used to play games like hopscotch and kiss chase − I've got a scar just above my left eye where I fell over and smashed my glasses while playing kiss chase. There was blood and glass everywhere and I was taken into the first-aid room, got it cleaned up and a plaster put on, then it was back to class. At home time they sent a note home with me to tell my parents what had happened.

How I came to be wearing glasses is that, within a few months of being in the school I discovered that I was short-sighted and couldn't see the blackboard, so I had to get glasses and wow! It was another world. My little glasses with the pink frames were great.

So, this particular day we were playing kiss chase with the girls running in one direction and the boys in another and I tripped and fell over. There was no big fuss or risk assessment like there would be now. It wasn't a big deal but the worse thing was that I smashed my lovely glasses and couldn't see for a few weeks until I got another pair.

Nefertiti: We were treated differently. I remember the name calling and being slapped on my legs by the teachers and told that I would never amount to anything. This was when I was about 12 or 13, and being compared to the Asian girls and told that they would turn out better than me. But I did have one white teacher that liked me when I went to college, and he inspired me to get into writing and poetry.

I did the usual stuff of telling my mother that I was going to the Catholic church and would end up at the Allardyce Club dancing and listening to the sound systems, so I became quite rebellious. I got pregnant when I was 15 and had to be taken into care and at 16 I was in college doing sociology and English literature 'O' levels. That's where my interest in poetry really began and I started to learn more about my identity and culture, which influenced a lot of my poems back then.

Maria: My enduring memory is of being "different" at that time was the name calling — on the streets, on the buses, everywhere you went: "wog", "coon", "n***er". But "black b****d" was their favourite, I think. Grown ups would just walk past and elbow you and call you a nasty name. On the bus they would say "only five standing" and you would be the one who had to get off. As a child, it's hard to take in.

Clearly we were different; we looked different, we're "not supposed to be here"; we're "taking things", we're here to "take things that don't belong to us". That's how we're being made to feel.

My parents were bus conductors and I was aware of the kind of abuse that they got on a regular basis and of the kind of things they had to do to signal to people: "Don't mess!" They would use their body language to let people know that if they abused them there would be repercussions so they'd better not even dare. And it worked. And there was a lot of camaraderie with the other people; you didn't leave your comrades in a position where they were going to be attacked. Your antenna was always up because if anything was happening you had to run since you were always out-numbered. So, people had always to be on their guard.

In those days, locally, everybody (black Caribbean people) knew everybody, more or less, and people looked out for one another.

Maria says: "This is dedicated to the memory of my parents, Mr & Mrs I A Richards — Ivan & Hyacinth — and to the memory of Mother Dear and Mother Lara, my beloved grandmothers."

WINNIFRED BYER

*From Jamaica, she trained and worked
in nursing before retiring.*

I came to England in March 1961 by plane, and I remember that we stopped in Canada because the weather was so bad and we had to transfer from the plane to a building. That was the first time I had ever seen snow, and it was so thick and cold. All I had on was a light dress but they gave us blankets, so it wasn't too bad. We were there for about four hours and then we got back on the plane.

My two eldest brothers were living here then, and the year before I came up another one came over to join them. They wrote to me and invited me over and I remember I had a dream before I left Jamaica; a dream that I was in England. That was even before anybody wrote to me with the idea of going to England. People were travelling abroad all the time, but I never really gave it much thought for myself until when I had that dream.

When I came, it wasn't as cold as I had expected. I suppose that was because it was almost spring. I was living with my brothers in north London for about three months before I applied to do nursing and was invited for an interview. I travelled all the way from Camden, in north London, to Croydon in Surrey, to the interview at Queen's Hospital. It was a long journey on different buses, but it wasn't a problem. In those days you just did whatever you had to do to get on.

The interview itself wasn't bad and they asked some questions about general knowledge and current affairs, like, who was the Prime Minister? It was Macmillan and I knew that from Jamaica. The test was OK and I passed it. The interview was held at the nursing school and it was just like the dream I'd had in Jamaica before I came — even the place where the interview happened was just the same as in the dream.

I was 29 at the time and all of them were surprised that I looked so good for my age. I was slightly older than everyone else, who were going on 20, 21, 22. When I came here some people said I looked like Princess Margaret. My hair was short and I had a dimple and high cheek bones. I didn't think I looked anything like the Queen's sister, but that was just what they said. But, you should have seen some of the girls in those days. Talk about pretty! Some of the girls from St Lucia, St Vincent, those different islands were just so beautiful. You could see that they were natural beauties, and if you could see the way they carried themselves! Well, let's just say they would turn heads in those days, but from some of them started putting on make-up and staying out late at parties they just spoiled their looks. As for me, I just used a little Nivea moisturising cream to keep my skin nice and clear. That was all; I don't believe in using make-up.

When I was training to be a nurse some of us were

treated badly on the job, but we had to take it. All of us student nurses had to go to Purley, in Surrey, to a geriatric hospital for general training lasting for six months and they could be very prejudiced there. But, when I went for the first time I almost gave up the nursing — not because of the treatment but because it was so cold.

I was in a department treating infectious diseases and they had two patients in one cubicle and the area was so cold right out by the open corridor. It was hell; talk about cold! And the winter was so bad — that was in 1962. A year later in 1963 we had the big freeze, when it was even colder.

I got as far as to write a letter of resignation to the matron and she called me the office and asked me why I had done that. She told me how much it had cost to train me and to write letters to Jamaica for references, so I told her that I would stay on. And it was a good thing that I did because in the long run it has paid off.

We don't have bad winters again nowadays. What we have now is nothing compared to what it was like in the '60s. I think it is because the scriptures are being fulfilled; because so many strangers from warm lands came here to live, the Lord has changed the weather. It has to be! I can't tell when last I wore winter shoes but, in those days you had to wear winter shoes and thick coats; thick, thick winter clothes all the time.

At work, we did have some experiences that weren't so nice. As a pupil nurse I wasn't always given the chance to learn as much as I should have done. For example, I didn't always get to go to theatre to learn new things although some others got the chance. You would feel it but you couldn't fight it; you just did what you could do. They would hold you back if they could and, because you missed out on those opportunities, it meant that you missed the full benefits of the training.

As an SEN (State Enrolled Nurse) my training took two years while the SRN (State Registered Nurse) training took three years. I just decided to settle for SEN, although, when I graduated, I could have put in another two years and done the SRN.

The uniform was a lime green dress, white apron and white cap, and we also had a nurse's cape, which was navy blue with red lining. We always looked smart. The matrons, home sisters and ward sisters would never have allowed us to have a hair out of place, anyway, but we did take great pride in our appearance and in our work.

Hospitals were always clean in those days, not like now when you have all these managers making a fuss over nothing but the hospitals are filthy and patients can get sick from the dirty conditions. It was never like that in our days, no way. I don't know why they got rid of the matrons, although some of them were strict. They were concerned about better conditions and the system worked much better back then.

Well, I was confident that I would pass my exams and I did. Funnily enough, I had a dream before the exams, and in the dream I saw what was going to happen on the day; what subjects would come up. When I awoke from the dream, I decided to study hard on those subjects, and, sure enough, on the day, the very subjects that I had dreamed about came up. Could you imagine?

The assessors came from the General Nursing Council and we had to do our practicals in pairs. We were tested on demonstrating things like doing a bed bath or removing stitches.

I worked with a girl from Guyana. The two of us were very particular in the assessment, doing everything in great detail and we got a lot of encouragement from the assessors. We did the practical and nursing theory, and, three months later, we got our results. I graduated and stayed in that profession until I retired, although, towards the end I transferred from nursing to a part-time role doing housekeeping at the hospital where I had worked during my career. I didn't marry and start a family until after I had finished my studying. I met my future husband, Oscar, through an uncle of mine who was living in the area. It turned out that he attended some of my uncle's church fellowships, so uncle got to find out what sort of person he was.

I was a Christian too and once, after I had gone to their church for Bible study, he offered to walk me home. On the way, he made his intentions clear: he was interested in marriage. I told him that I would think about it. Three years later, after I had graduated as a student nurse, we were married.

If I hadn't done the nursing, I would have wanted to do book-keeping but since that didn't work out I stuck with nursing. In those days, it was only £1.50 for the year to do a course at Croydon College. I wanted to do geography and maths, which I started to do in the evenings, but I couldn't keep it up because of the nursing. I loved maths and was good at it, but I couldn't continue the studies as I worked full-time.

I have never been "home sick". When I came to this country I didn't have any idea how long I would be here but I've been here now for over 40 years. I didn't really experience any bad treatment when I came to England. There were a few incidents but you had to tolerate them for the Lord's sake and, sometimes it was your own people who gave you a hard time. We hardly speak about it but that is the truth; sometimes your own can try and keep you back. People would put pressure on you to try and make you leave your job and I had to tell them that I wasn't going to leave until I was ready. All those things happened and you had to be strong to pass through them.

EDNA*

*Retired from her clerical job but does voluntary work.
From Jamaica but she had originally intended to go to
the United States.*

Back home, on certain days, we usually marched with our flags and we would sing, "God save the King", and things like that. So, when I came here in 1962, it was a bit of a shock. I landed at Gatwick airport. There was this little house (the terminal building) and just open fields and I was expecting a better airport than that.

Coming to London, I saw all these chimneys and I thought they were all factories. I came here to my uncle and his wife, and came to learn nursing but that winter was very difficult. I could do shorthand and I could type, and I tried a few places to get office work but I didn't get a job anywhere, so I went to do machining, which was still hard to get into, but I continued until I got work and I got experience and I could move about and find my way around.

But there was a lot of prejudice in the factories, on the street, even in the churches, which we weren't expecting. I never came across it because I didn't go to church straight away, but I knew people who went to Church of England churches and the ministers asked them not to come back because the white congregations didn't feel comfortable with them.

After that, I didn't even go to Church of England, which was my church from back home, I went to a church at Finsbury Park, in north London, where they were mixed and then I got more confidence. Still, Church of England started to spill over and I think some of the whites started moving out of the churches (laughs) because today there are more black people in the church than white; Church of England or anywhere.

So, the prejudice was very, very strong, and still is, even today, but now we can deal with it because we know what to expect. But I never went around with a chip on my shoulder.

To get work in the '60s, you mostly had to know somebody who was working somewhere and they asked the manager on your behalf. But, for you to just go in and ask for a vacancy, that wasn't really the way.

I came across a lot of rejection, although I could do what they were doing. I didn't give up, though, I continued and worked my way then went to night school and I did private training and ended up working for a local council, in social services, which had a lot of prejudice as well — you find it everywhere — but you just learned to deal with certain things.

Your workload would be more than certain people's in your same stage and when you could get promoted to a higher grade, I think you were kept back; things like that. Oh, God! In these places they say there's no prejudice but there is; it's hidden.

Entertainment

The music was good and there were a lot of parties. There wasn't so much drugs as what is on the scene now. So, we enjoyed ourselves and we were good movers (laughs). I especially used to like the American jazz; you could really bop to that.

I can remember one time in the '60s we were going to a party and we were in a car and the car stopped at the lights and we were abused by three white youths. They were shouting racial abuse and threatening us, but when the lights changed we drove off. We weren't the type to just pick a fight. It's best to walk away at times.

Am I going back to live in the West Indies? Well, I have retired now so why should I leave? I've put my youth, my skills, my labour into this country. I have to get back some of what I put into the system. That's it.

* Not her real name. Interviewee preferred not to be identified.

TOM EVANS

A shoemaker and father of 10 from Jamaica.

I came in 1963. It was rotten, very rotten. I was really disappointed because the things that I had learned about England, I didn't see them. I learned that England was paved with gold and London was built on the River Thames, but when I came here it was different thing altogether.

I saw the houses with chimneys. I never saw that before in my life, so I thought they were all factories. Well, I didn't stumble when I got here because somebody knew that I was coming and prepared a job for me. But it wasn't nice.

When I got the first pay packet, I cried from the factory at Angel Road in Islington, straight home to where I was living at Anthill Road in Tottenham. I was crying because the wages that I got was not even one clip of the money I made from the bananas I used to grow, cut and sell back home in Jamaica. I got paid six pounds at the job when I first came, and I cried so much that when I went home my wife asked me what was wrong. I couldn't tell her, I just handed her the pay packet. And she opened it and said, "Is this why you are crying? Don't be so sad, it will get better." But I packed up my things and decided to go back home. And she said, "You're going home and leaving me?"

I said, "Yes".

Well, I went to book my fare with the intention that after a month staying here, I would go, but at the time I booked I found myself in trouble. My wife was pregnant and I couldn't leave her. So, I couldn't go again. I had to decide to stay. I had left children back home so I just sent for them and I stayed here. We went on and on for a good while.

At the factory where I worked, I had a big room where I worked by myself. The paymaster for the factory — I was going to kill him. What happened was, one pay day they sent and called me, and when I went I saw some money on the table and my heart went bump. I said to the paymaster, "Yes, you wanted to show me something?"

As he started to take up the pay packet I asked, "Is it my money?" He said, "Yes".

I told him, "You can't open my pay packet before so many people." It was disrespectful.

Then I told him "It's a mad world" and I walked off and left them. The supervisor was near to me and I went and complained to him, but, later, the paymaster came up with a tray with money in it and as he went to pass he chopped me in my stomach. And I held him. There were about 20 black men in there and they said, "Evans, don't do it!" So I loosed him and let him go.

In those days, you had to have a National Insurance number if you were leaving that job you had to get your card so that you could get a job somewhere else. I asked them for my card and they refused to give it to me. They said, "Not you, we don't want you to leave."

They had this factory and couldn't get anybody to do the work, and after I came they fell in love with me, saying that I was doing the work properly and so on. And they wouldn't give me my card, but I left the job because every time I saw the man (the paymaster) I got vexed.

Well, it was a unionised factory and the union secretary and the chairman came and said they were going to take the case to court because the man shouldn't have hit me. But I wasn't satisfied, I felt like killing him. Yes, honestly. I shouldn't use those words now but it is true. And they sent for a lawyer and when the lawyer came to take a statement, everybody said they didn't see what happened.

So, I said, "Well!"

They couldn't pursue the case because they had no witnesses and no evidence.

Housing

It was very difficult in those days trying to find somewhere to live. When I came here, my wife got a room from a Bajan man, very nice fellow. But I didn't stay there any time at all because it didn't suit me. It was only one room and I had my children in Jamaica and I wanted to send for them. Although the work here wasn't nice, I did have a few shillings with me so I decided to bring them over.

I was looking to get a place with at least three rooms and in most of the paper shops you would see them advertising flats for rent and when you'd go and knock they would say "It's gone", although it wasn't so. Or else, you got some places where they would ask if you had children. If you said yes, they'd say, "Sorry, we can't take you." And that was the time that it was very rotten.

Anyway, I got a house from a Jew man and he said,

"Why not buy it?" I said that I didn't have money to buy it. He said, "The same money you pay me for rent can buy it."Then he said he would give me a mortgage and so I took it. I wasn't a rich man but I could find at least two shillings. I'd sent for the children but life still wasn't so nice. Anyway, I took the house and one day I came home and there was an elderly white man in the house.

I asked, "What do you want?"

He said, "The government has sent me to take over the house." I said, "You're joking."

He said, "No, the house is under compulsory purchase order and the owner of the house has got paid for it already." And he gave me two weeks to leave the place. I said, "You must be mad!"

Well, that was in 1965, something like that. Oh, Lord, it was too much. Labour was in power and I wrote to Mr Wilson, the Prime Minister. He wrote back and said, "Sit down there and make yourself happy."

Then, one morning about two months afterwards, as I was going to work, a man drove up and said he had a key and he was going to show me a house, so I must call my wife. And he took us to the house. It was clean and nice so I took it. At that time, houses didn't value anything because the first house that I bought had six bedrooms and two bathrooms, kitchen and sitting room. And I paid £4,500 for it. Now, you'd have to pay about £100,000!

Church

I had a very rough time in church. I think it was a Church of England church I visited when I came here. I went in there and after the service the parson asked me not to come back. They didn't want you in there because you were a black man, and they said that you weren't their member and that the white people never liked to see you. All those sorts of ignorant things.

When I heard that I felt like dying because that was saying you weren't good enough for them. They claimed themselves better than you. They weren't Christians; if they were Christians they wouldn't tell you that. But, we survived till now.

Teddy Boys

Once, I got into trouble with some Teddy Boys. I had gone up Amhurst Road in Hackney, east London, to look for a school mate of my wife and when I was coming back that night I saw six of them coming down the road. And me and them get into hot water because me a pass go 'bout me business and them want to beat me.

I fought them because, at that time, I was young and strong and I had just come from Jamaica. After they found that they couldn't manage me, they ran. I mean, if I didn't defend myself they would beat me, kill me, but I had a knife and I held one and I stick him! And he fell on the ground and all of them ran off.

At first I wasn't going to the police but I met a nurse and I was telling her what had happened and she said that I should go to the station. I told her that they may arrest me, but, anyway, I went and told them what happened. The police went to the area but they didn't see the man. He was gone, so I went about my business and never heard anything more about it again.

RENNIE MILLER

Retired payroll supervisor from Jamaica.

I came in 1960 and with what I had heard about England, I was disappointed; very much disappointed and I said I was only staying for a year.

The situation here wasn't nice. It was pretty rough. I came to my brother and we were all here and things were not running the way I wanted it. Then my mother died in Jamaica and I held on.

Well, what I had heard about England, I don't know if it was a rumour but they said it was paved with gold (laughs) and that the people were nice but I found that totally wrong.

Getting accommodation was hard. To get a room, they put the sign up, "Sorry no blacks, no Irish". They always said that. You would see the sign, "Room available", but when you'd go and ask for it, they'd say, "It's gone".

The jobs were the same. I went to London Transport, but they turned me down. I came here to be an accountant. I had gone to one company and asked about a job (doing accountancy). The manager said, "Sorry, Mr Miller, the job is here but it's not for a coloured." He told me bluntly. I was disappointed, so I went back to London Transport.

The manager gave me a form and I filled it out to the best of my ability. All that was asked I answered. At the end of the day he said, "Sorry, you have to go to the kitchen to work." And I was annoyed and I said something that wasn't nice to him for wasting my time; making me carry all my qualifications and all they were offering was for me to go and work in the kitchen, so I said, "No!" I didn't want to do that.

Of course, I was heartbroken. That's why I was disappointed when I came here. I thought about going back home, definitely. For, if my mother didn't pass away, straight away I would have gone back. For, hearing about what it is (England) and coming to see for myself was something totally different.

Eventually, I got on to a Jewish firm. I was the only black there and it was like a supervision post, for he took me on, then he would take me to the bank to sign the cheques and draw money to pay the workers — which they weren't too happy about.

But, you know, I wasn't stepping down from that job, because what I wanted, I couldn't get it. And I decided not to come here to sweep the street or to do things below my dignity, for I didn't do it back home so I didn't see why I should come here and set down lower.

Eventually, after a while, I got on well with them. We had a few bust-ups, yes, for they would take liberties with me and I'm one that I don't stand any nonsense. I will tell you there and then what I think of you. For example, the foreman, first thing he came to me and said, "You black bastard, go and wash the van!" And I didn't like it, so I took him upstairs.

I said, "Come, let's go upstairs here."

We went into a room and I shut the door. Then I gave him what for! Calling me a black bastard!

I said, "I'm not a van boy." And he didn't like it. When I held him and struck him, he started bleeding. I thought they were going to lock me up, you know. And he wasn't pleased about it.

Anyway, I was in a rage and, because I had locked the door, he started hammering on the door and the others came to find out what was happening. He went down and told the boss what I did and the boss wanted to know why I did that so I told him and the fellow admitted that he'd called me a black bastard and said he was sorry. Some time afterwards he came and said, "Rennie, let us be friends."

He was in the job for 14 years but after that incident (after I gave him what for), within less than six months he left. Yes. But what happened, why they didn't like it was because I was the only black man there and I got the supervisor's job to go and sign cheques and draw money. Not to give them orders, just to see to it that everything ran all right. They didn't like that, for they didn't want to take orders from a black person. I was disappointed, as I said before.

Well, things have changed now and meeting the other people, the other islanders — that I had never met before — was a high point. We had heard of them and we read about them in school but never met them, and when we did meet, we got on all right. But, mainly with the whites, I never really got on with them, for as I said I don't stand for nonsense. I'm very outspoken. If I am with you, I am with you but if you tell me things that I don't like, I'm very hasty — I'll give you what for!

It wasn't pleasant living in one room. When you look at it, the cooking facilities weren't good and the bathing facilities weren't good either. Compared to the facilities I had back home, when I came here it was totally different. I wasn't happy at all, and if my mother had lived a year or two more, I wouldn't be here now, I'd have gone back right away. I'm not the only child but I was mother's pet, you know, and I had things cushy and nice.

Plus, when I came here in January it was winter. I had never seen snow or fog before. And going out you had to be rubbing your hands and you had to put on that heater to get a little bit warm. I drank a little of the white rum and put on a lot of clothes to try and keep myself warm sometimes. I gained a lot of experience coming here but it has not been so nice.

Entertainment

We met friends from other islands and we'd go from house to house. One week you'd go to them and then the next week they came by you and it would go around. That's how we would meet and socialise. We would go to the shebeen*, you know, and enjoy ourselves.

At that time they would have, call it a radiogram (record player), and they'd have all the latest records. You'd put on the records and enjoy yourself and you'd eat and drink, and dance and laugh until it was time to finish.

When Millie Small sang, "My Boy Lollipop", that was very exciting. I like calypso, I like samba, I liked most of them old-time music and, well, our parties were actually all night in those days.

Well, at the place where I was staying they said by 10 o'clock you had to be in. And I was accustomed to being out all night back home, you hear, so when the person said to me, "Be in by ten", I said, "No way, I'm not coming in so early."

After two weeks, I left and found another room to rent. The place where I went to stay had no restrictions, so I could come and go as I liked.

* *Shebeens were house parties / dances. People paid to go in and they were usually crowded out. Shebeen is a Jamaicanised version of "shove in". In other words, "make room; lots more people coming in to party."*

GLORIA EVANS

*Now an octogenerian, she came from
Jamaica and insists she only came for five years.*

My baby daughter was five months old when I came to England in May 1961. Unfortunately, I had to leave her behind with my mother. My husband was there with the rest of the family, including the other children, so it was all right, but nonetheless a hard decision to make. He and I had agreed that we would both go to England, but I left Jamaica before him.

I know it is quite something to decide to leave your country and a new baby behind to try and make a new life in a strange country, but you have to understand that things in Jamaica were very hard, and where we were in the countryside was really rough. You know what country gives? At that time it was mostly hardship and everyone was struggling. I wasn't working and although my husband was a shoemaker and did his cultivating, things were still tough. The new baby was our sixth child and we were all trying our best to eke out a living. Going to England seemed like an opportunity of a lifetime; a chance to make a better life with prospects for our young h family, and that was what made me leave.

Like everyone else, I had heard stories about what England was like and imagined that it was beautiful. I was naïve, and of course I was glad to get the chance to leave my little island and come away for a better life; better prospects. Anyway, all we needed to travel out of Jamaica back then was our passport and the fare because the country was still under British rule. So, at that time, we could come and go without any difficulty.

I had an aunt who had her own house in Islington, north London, so I stayed with her when I first came. My impressions, apart from the fact that I had never experienced such cold weather in my life, was that I looked around and I thought to myself, "Where is everybody?" It seemed as if no one lived here because you didn't see anyone in their gardens, you hardly saw anyone on the streets; all you saw were the houses. For a city, the place seemed very desolate.

My first job was working in a canteen at the same place as my aunt; she got me the job. I did that for about six months and then decided to go into nursing. The governor, the manager of the canteen, gave me a beautiful reference. He said, "Gloria, if you fail, it's your own fault. You have a lot going for you so make the most of it."

When I came, nursing was one of the easiest things to get into, although I had always loved teaching and used to do some teaching back home. When I got accepted for the nursing that sort of decided it. So, I got a job in a hospital and moved out of my aunt's place and lived in the nurses' home until my husband, Tom, came to join me in 1963. By 1964, I was pregnant, '65, I was pregnant,

'66, I was pregnant and our last child came in the '70s.

Anyway, I packed up full-time nursing and worked part-time, doing nights, as a Nursing Assistant at Claybury psychiatric hospital in Woodford Green, Essex.

It was easier for me to look after the children during the day while my husband was at work, and then go and do my work when he came home in the evenings. Yes, it was tiring and demanding, but that is just how it was.We weren't the only ones doing that. Some had to hold down full-time jobs and send their children out to child-minders, so at least we managed to work it out for ourselves.

I kept that job at the mental hospital for 13 years until I retired. I suppose that's why I now have so much trouble sleeping at night! Anyway, we moved home several times, as the family grew and we decided to send for the children who were back home.

If I weren't so maternal, I wouldn't have put my own dreams and ambitions on the back-burner to focus on my family. I might have been able to do both: have a career and a family, but like a lot of mothers I sacrificed for my family and now that everyone's flown the nest I am trying to find myself again.

I love to write and I enjoy painting, but never had the chance to really do those things. Every time I thought I could try and follow my own plans, something came up and I sacrificed to help others. That has been the story of my life. I feel as though I have lost me, and I don't know where I've gone.

At one point, when the children had finished their education, I could have gone back home but as time went on it became harder and harder to make the move and eventually sickness set in so we were caught in a dilemma. It would be hard now to try and settle back home having lived here for so long — longer than I spent in Jamaica — so I don't see myself being there permanently, although I long to go and visit.

I am feeling a little restless but the big issue now is poor health, which stops a lot of things in its tracks because my health is deteriorating and I can't move about as independently as I would like.

The funny part about it was that I actually came to England for five years. I know a lot of people claim that, but it was really my plan. I wanted to do my training and go back home to open a children's home. Sadly, that never happened and I doubt it will happen now.

Consolation

Nothing seems to console you much today,
Of which, I am so sorry to hear and see;
But Jesus, before his crucifixion journey,
Was himself troubled, very much indeed;
He took aside three of his closet friends,
To watch, abide and pray with him awhile;
But they fell asleep, because the flesh is weak.

'Though on this path of life things can go amiss,
God, in mercy, sends comfort when we're weak,
Keep looking up, dear, the Saviour is still here;
We cannot see him, but his presence we can feel;
Regardless of condition, he is a true consolation;
Don't be discouraged, your guardian angel's near,
Because he is timeless, he will deliver you on time.

© 2009. Gloria Evans

JEAN*

*In her seventies. She came to the UK from
Montserrat in 1960.*

I came on the first of September and my impression
was, I didn't think it was like how I had heard, but
after I came here and got used to it I found it not so
difficult.

I had heard that England was cold and foggy but I
never heard about gold here like some people did. I
just heard that England was not a bad place and it was
easy to get a job. I had never heard that the people were
friendly, never, but I expected them to be better, some of
them.

As soon as I came I lived with my cousin and after
that I got a room which was a very difficult situation,
being that you were not used to living that way back
home.

You lived in one room and you were sharing one
kitchen, one bath – some of them never even had a bath.

But I got a job as soon as I came, and I worked from there until when I retired. I was a machinist first, and then after that I got a job in another department which made light bulbs and lighting. Then I got a job in a hospital.

In the early days it wasn't bad, you know what I mean? You worked with people; you worked with white and you worked with black. Sometimes you were having more problems with the blacks than the whites, but we all pulled together and we got along.

I didn't have any enemies in my workplace. I more had it (trouble) where I was living with my own black people; my own coloured people! So many disagreements, sometimes over petty little things.

I remember once or twice I had the feeling that I wanted to go back to Montserrat but as the years went by you got to know people and you got to mix, you had a job and money was coming in. I never think, well, I would go back right away, but I would go back for a holiday, and I went back to my country three times for a holiday.

Black people made a lot of contributions over the years. They helped to build up this country, because a lot of black people worked hard for what they got in our days. Not like now.

* Not her real name. Interviewee preferred not to be identified.

JOYCE DOUGLAS

*Came from Jamaica with her parents as a
16 year-old in 1957.*

Some of them would ask you the time because they thought that we read the time from the sun; that you didn't use your watch; you told the time from the sky.

And, you know, we always found it very, very funny because we used to tell the time back home from the sun; when the sun goes down or it goes up. But they believed when we came to this country we did the same thing and the white people always thought it funny and they called us "black monkey".

"Oh, look at that one with the tail — she's a monkey", or, "He's a black bastard". It was very, very, very insulting for we black people that came to England in 1957. It was very, very bad.

I worked in a factory, doing sewing and I tried to do different types of things until I got married in 1958, then I started a family. You always had to stay in one room and, if you had your child, they wouldn't rent you a place.

If you went and knocked at the door and you asked for a room, they closed the door in your face and told you, "Get away you black bastard or monkey", or something like that. It was really, really bad, you know.

When we first came to England and saw the buses with the tram running to pull the bus along, what they call it? Oh, Lord, it's like a tram, yes, overhead, where the bus is hooked on to (trolleybus) just going on and on and you're going to work in the morning. Everybody's rushing to go to work. If the bus broke down you would have to sit there until they got someone to take it off the pole. Oh, it was really terrible.

And, then, you could just imagine — it was very, very cold. Very, very, very cold. You had to wear a lot of clothes, and pad up yourself as best you could, because we were used to the heat, you see. But you had to wear all these long johns, down to your ankles, like trousers, then you had on your skirt. Oh, it's a lot that we've been through.

I was very homesick. Many times I would tell my father, "I want to go back home. I wish I could go back home." Really and truly, then, to go back home without my parents, that I would have found a bit difficult because I was still young when I came and I didn't get to know England much anyway. So, I decided to stay and give it a chance until, eventually, I pulled through.

What you had was a cold country and very cold-hearted people. They were very cold. You know, it was only in 1958, '59 or '60, coming up then, that everything changed and they tried to be nice. But you still got that prejudice, you know, and they still called you "black bastard", they didn't get away from that, or the monkey — "Monkey there on the street".

People used to get into fights. We usually had trouble from Teddy Boys. Once, I was on the street coming from work at Stamford Hill, walking down in the bright nice evening, and about six of them ganged up on me. They wanted to take my bag and such, threatening me and I remember I was wearing a tall-heeled shoes (high heels) and I just stood up in the street like I was lost. I took off one of the shoes after a while and held it in my hand and I shouted, "I'm going to *****ing kill you!" And they ran off.

That was the last time any of them ever approached me. You know, a lot of black people got killed and mugged and all sorts of thing that we heard about.

The first job I had in this country was at Tottenham Court Road in central London. I was only working for about four pounds a week after tax and everything, and I had to give some to my parents for my keep.

At that time, you could buy clothes, shoes, oh yes, oh yes, pay your rent, all right, and you still had money left over. That was nice. Not like now: you buy a cup of coffee and a sandwich now and it costs you £4!

By the time I came home from work in the evening it was dark and miserable. While you were at work, they (co-workers) would give you bad eyes and taunt you: "You black bastard!"

If you asked any question, they ignored you, but you still had to get on with your job and they were usually quick to sack you. The least little thing you did they were ready to fire you. It was very, very hard to live here; they picked on you for nothing. You didn't have to do anything for the white man to tell you, "Oh, get off you black bastard" or that you had to go. No respect at all, just the least mistake you made they'd fire you, but you could easily get another job.

At that time, you could walk out of one job and into the next job. You could have three or four jobs for the day, if you could do them, because I've done it. If I was working with you and you said, "You're fired!" All right, I'd just walk out and I'd go next door and start working again. That is how I usually did it.

I did have friends. I tried to make friends with different black people who came from different countries, like Barbados or St Kitts or anything like that. We all tried to unite together when we met for company or to make friends the best we could.

When I was a kid back home in Jamaica, I was always day-dreaming about travelling. I always wished I could travel and get to know different places. And, eventually, I had to come to England. Up to now I've always wanted to travel the world, if I had the money.

I think we black people have changed a lot of things in this country, even for nursing; everything. We made changes because, when I came in this country to be honest with you, they would give you fish and chips in newspaper, and you would see bread on the door-step from in the morning until at night when people were coming from work. A dog would go and piss on it and they'd still come home, take it up and make sandwiches and everything — ah, no, no. It was shocking, you know. It was horrible.

Now, we can walk more freely and do things; it's much better. But, living-wise, it's harder now because things are more expensive.

PETER WHITE

*Born in Montserrat, he went for army training in Jamaica,
and later travelled to England in 1958 from Curaçao on
a boat called "The Queen of the Sea".*

During the war, I was a corporal in the British army and had the opportunity to travel all over the Caribbean on duty or exercise, spending a good deal of time in Antigua and Jamaica.

When the war ended, I again travelled from island to island working as a refinery worker with companies like Shell Oil Company. I worked with Shell for 13 years and when the contract ended, I decided to come to England, the "Mother Country".

Everything pointed me in this direction because, in the army, I had made friends with English boys. We would have put our necks on the block for each other, we were so close. Also, the island where I was born, Montserrat, was a British territory and so there were a lot of connections with this country. However, when I came and saw the scale of things, I got such a shock.

We docked at Southampton on a cold, blowy (windy) day in September. Seeing the smoke coming from the houses, I thought they were on fire. And, later on, seeing fire inside the houses was something strange. The paraffin and coal fires were a problem because they made your clothes smell awful and, also, they caused many of us to get bronchitis and asthma. Yet, we survived.

I had a brother living in Harlesden and lived there with him for a time. Later on, I moved around to different areas, settling in Notting Hill. I went to get a job on a building site but it was so cold and miserable doing the outdoor work that after that one day on the job I did not return, not even to collect the day's pay. Instead, I got a job at Olympia Exhibition Centre, working in the kitchens, which was handy since I ate all my meals there.

I had a room in Ladbroke Grove, which cost 10 shillings a week. It was hard for a young man like myself feeling so contained in such a small space with so many rules to live by. I was used to freedom but, now, I felt like an animal in a cage.

In the 1960s, the racialists started to move in. Sir Oswald Moseley was rallying his group against the Jews and now they were also turning their hatred to the blacks and the Irish. We were put in one category: "No Irish, no blacks, no dogs".

Eventually, Enoch Powell began making his speeches about "Rivers of Blood", yet, he had been the minister who had gone to the Caribbean pleading on bended knees for our prime ministers to send workers to this country.

Our young women came as nurses, especially looking after war victims. We came here in peace and love. The police had no worries from us; we had had a good up-bringing and yet, when we came, we found so much hostility against us.

The Teddy Boys got every encouragement from Sir Oswald Moseley. They used to wear their flashy suits and slicked their hair back with Brylcreem. And, they would attack any black person who was on his own but they were cowards and wouldn't dare attack groups of blacks.

We decided that our backs were against the wall, so we got together as ex-soldiers, ex-RAF and ex-police from the Caribbean to fight back. At that time, Notting Hill was right in the heart of the tension, and more than one of our boys was killed because of racialism.

Whenever we went into the pubs, they would stare at us with so much hatred, but they couldn't attack us. I was six foot odd, weighing sixteen-and-a-half stones and my nickname was "Big Peter", so they weren't going to take a chance and come and attack me.

Late one night, a chap I knew was walking through Ladbroke Grove when he met a gang of six Teddy Boys. He couldn't run to the left because there was a train line and he could have got killed trying to cross it. If he ran to the right, they were bound to chase and catch him. He felt like he was dead now, so he dropped on his knees and started to pray out loud:

"Oh, Lord, me kill six people in Jamaica and me granny tell me not to kill any more people when me come to England but it look like me have six more fi kill right now. Please no mek me kill them."

When he opened his eyes, all the Teddy Boys had ran off! We enjoyed that one for a long time afterwards, I tell you. But, it was to the shame of the British Government that we went through all that because they invited us to this country.

I remember Norman Manley, Jamaica's Prime Minister, coming over here and telling the British Government that they had called us here and we had come to work honestly but we were encountering problems of racialism, which was set to destroy us.

Another bad point was that we had to do the worse and dirtiest jobs alongside the Irish, who were digging up the streets and doing the building work.

No one has ever apologised to us, even to this day. The government of this country owes us an apology for the way we were called here only to be trodden into the dumps. The racialism we faced was institutionalised; it wasn't just a matter of individuals here and there, it was ingrained in the whole society.

Marrying an English girl

When I met my wife, who is English, I had gone into a shop one day to buy some onions and I asked a lady how much they were and she said she didn't work there. Well, we left at the same time and I held the door for her and we just got talking. I asked if I could see her again and she said yes, so we exchanged phone numbers.

About two weeks later, I called her and we made a date. But the way the society was, we faced so much hatred and opposition because black and white were not supposed to go out, marry and have kids together. People were always saying, "It will never work", and "It's the children I feel sorry for."

I remember going to see Margaret's — my girlfriend's — parents down at Bournemouth. After a while, she went off into the bedroom for a talk with her mum and I was left having a drink and a chat with her dad. I thought to myself, "If Margaret comes out with a smile on her face, then I'm in, if not, then that's it, I'm not accepted."

Well, when she came out she was grinning from ear to ear so I knew that I was welcomed as part of the family. Her mother put her arm around me and said, "From now on, call me Mum."

My own family also had doubts because mixed

relationships were not agreeable in this country, but when we travelled to Montserrat my mum said the same thing to Margaret as her mum had said to me, "Call me Mum."

We have been married for over 40 years now and we still hold hands walking down the street and we holiday together. We love each other as if we just met. The secret is togetherness; you've got to give and take, share and share alike. We have five children and they are all happily married to people from different backgrounds. Our family could even be called "The United Nations".

MILDRED DEACON

From St Catherine, Jamaica. Came to England in 1963 and lived in Manchester before moving to London.

My first thought was, "Oh, I'm going to get a job. I must get a job, because there's a lot of factories here", since I saw the smoke coming from the roofs. But, later, I found out they were houses, not factories. And, I was really shocked by everything. I cried night and day to go back, but I couldn't.

I hated it because, according to the situation, you had no fridge here in those days. you had to put the jelly on the window-sill, and when you cooked the rice and peas for three days, you had to put it on the window-sill to keep fresh. If you went to the shop you had to buy things that could serve you for the whole week. On top of that, you didn't understand the country and it wasn't nice.

But, at least it was very cheap during them times. The food wasn't too bad because you could get the same

Jamaican food and it wasn't expensive like now. I would always buy a big cock chicken for five shillings, which we now call 25 pence, that could serve everybody. And, five pounds could provide dinner for 13 of us. Yet, now, I am on my own and I am spending over sixty, seventy pounds a week for food. Nowadays, you carry a twenty pound and go out, as you break the twenty pounds there's nothing left.

The first time I went to get a job I was pregnant and it was terrible. I went to a factory where they made the square cushions. I had to turn out the four corners of the cushion covers. And, because I was the only black there, they laughed at me night; they laughed day, and I never went back there. I only worked the one day and up till now I don't get that one day's pay because I never went back to that job.

They were laughing at me because I was a pregnant single woman and I was the only black between hundreds and thousands of whites. Whenever they found that you were a single person − and especially being pregnant − you is nothing. You is nothing...

In them days, they never wanted no black people to work with them. And I never went back to that job, nor did I get that one day's pay. No, I'll never forget that day. I couldn't even find my way when I was going home, and I had to walk because there was no bus running in that area of Manchester.

I lived in Manchester when I came, and then I got married and lived there for 21 years before my husband died. After he died, I went to live in London.

Well, I find it a bit better now, although I want to go home (to Jamaica) every day. It is because of my eyes (she is partially sighted) why I don't go.

I came to England to work because my boyfriend was here and I had two kids for him, but when I came, I found out that he had a new woman. He would go to work and not come home for three days and I had just come in the country and I had no job. So, I had to travel from London to Manchester, to Clifton Street, where my sister lived (She's dead now), but up till now I haven't seen that man again. And one of the girls is 35 and one is 41 next month.

It was really tough because I rented a house and had to keep my cooking pots in the bedroom. You couldn't watch their (the landlord's) telly, you had to go in your own room and stay in there. And then I only had sheet and I had to keep on my coat to keep me warm.

When I bunked up to go to sleep at night, I had to draw the bed right up to the fire. Then I would get up in the morning and shake it and light it again. It wasn't like now, anyway, because now you don't have to use coal fire and those things, but it was terrible when I came here. I cried night and day.

I never knew what I was coming to. If I was getting £1.25.0 a week in Jamaica when I came here, I would be a rich woman; I wouldn't have needed to come here. When I was selling 25lbs of saltfish, 25lbs of flour, 25lbs of rice and about one dozen soft drinks from this corner to that corner (as a street trader) back home, I was making money and I'm sorry the day I ever left it and come here, because I would be a rich woman in Jamaica now.

But, when I came here, I did just come to help myself because I was young in those days and I had these two kids with that man. Things never worked out as I would have liked it and up until now I still regret that I came here.

SAMUEL ALLEN

*A keen boxer in his youth, he came from Montserrat
in 1959. He has taken early retirement from
work, due to ill health.*

It was cold and I couldn't see because I was coming
from a warm country to a cold country where there
is a lot of light to a cold country where it is almost
dark most of the time, so you couldn't see.

And, in this country there have been a lot of changes
because, now, the sun shines, but when we came here
first it was always dark; day, night, the light was on.

It was a shock, right, because all you could see were
a few lights and there were the houses. And then there
was a white thing in the shadow of the darkness: that is
the chimney-stack on top with the smoke coming out.
But, you see, I come from a country where we knew
nothing about those things.

Well, everyone said England is so-so and my brother
and them told me I must come and that was the reason

why I came. I used to go to America, by the way, Florida and so on, but my brother forced me to come up here.

When you went to get work there was a lot of work but you got some places marked "No blacks", right, and when you'd go for a room sometimes they said, "No blacks" — that's all.

Well, I had a little pull up with a lady one time. I deposited £3 for a room where she said to me that her husband was not in so I'd have to come back on the weekend when her husband would be there. But later I decided that I didn't want the room any more, I would find somewhere else. But when I went back she didn't want to give me back my money. They had to get four policemen! They phoned up and said, "There's a black giving some trouble here," and four big policemen came down to speak to us and when they found out the truth the lady had to give back the £3. She had tried to get me into trouble.

Oh, yes, you had a lot of prejudice. When you would go to the bus stop you could have been the first one at the bus stop and if a crowd came they would want you to get to the back, so you'd be last. You see, nowadays you can stand anywhere at the bus stop. First time, you couldn't stand anywhere at the bus stop, you had to stand up in line and if you came to go on the bus before them. They must go on the bus and then if there was seat left over you would get a seat, that's if you were lucky. A lot of black people couldn't stand it so we had a lot of fights.

I got into a fight one time after we went to bingo. It was the bingo house at Hackney Road. We went there and I missed one number which would win me £556, which was a lot of money in those days. When I found out that I'd lost, we left and went to the bus stop to go home. Them times we were used to standing up by the door, we couldn't have a seat or nothing.

So, this evening after bingo we were at the bus stop long before anyone because we had left early and then the crowd comes out and about three or four buses come up but they were full up, because what? Because what the people did was they'd come out of the bingo and they'd go down a few stops before and fill up the buses.

So, about four buses came, all full up. Anyhow, another bus came and they got on the bus and started telling us to get to the back. And this half-caste lady joined in. She said: "Look at me, I'm behind them and you all want them to go to the back of the bus when they were the first at the bus stop?" And they all told her to go back to her country. So, she said, "What country? I was born here." But that made them mad. They went on and they went on and they went on.The men weren't so bad. Some of them went upstairs so we went inside the lower deck, but all the women were on us all the time, cussing, cussing, cussing, cussing. So, when things got too hot on the bus, my friend had a silver comb (he made them where he worked: combs for dogs and horses) and he took all the teeth off one end, so it had a point.

Now, one man came down from the upper deck and saw my friend take the thing out of his pocket, right, and he jumped off the bus to call the police. It was one big row and everything. So, the policemen stopped us and searched every part of the bus looking for weapons but didn't find a knife. The man who had called the police said, "There's a big knife on the bus, six inches." He was lying, but I wouldn't let them search me. About ten policemen had to all give me their numbers before I let them search me. And, when they searched me, the man that called the police said to me, "Come on, let's go over into this field." He wanted us to have a fight, you know. Now, I used to do wrestling and boxing, so I said to him, "Look, if I go into the field with you, you'll never touch me." But he was down on me, down on me to fight, so I called one of the policemen and said, "You see this man is inviting me to fight. That man's belly is touching the ground, he'll never touch me, and, if I go out there and I kill him, the judge and the law of this country are going to hang me, right?" The policeman said "Yes". And he made everyone get away, even the man who wanted to fight, and took us home in the police car.

Relationships with white women

They were on the street. They were like that. They were calling you. It was like that. Even where we were working in the day, they would come there asking for money — some of them were poor, you know, really poor with kids. They'd ask for a shilling or two, something like that. No man, I didn't go with them (laughs). I just called them pound for four (A pound for four of them). It was five shillings for a white lady. If you wanted to get to meet one, they were on the street.

My first wages paid three shillings an hour when I started working. I was a wood-turner machinist in a factory making lampshades, guitars, electric guitars, and a whole heap of things. I was underage and you had to understand they wouldn't give you the full wages or whatever, but that wasn't bad; that was £7 a week and big men were getting about eight, nine, ten pounds or so, that's all. And, as quick as I became 21, I leave it, man. They were going to make me foreman, but I gone because the other firm where I was going paid about four and six more. When you say four and six, that's about twenty-five pence now. Yeah, twenty-five! You could get fish and chips for nine pence and two pence chips, right, and you could get your bus fare for three pence. And when I say three pence, it's for a long distance, and if it's too long then you paid four pence. So, there is a lot of difference to how things are right now.

EDWIN MYERS

From Jamaica. Retired bus conductor, in his early seventies.

I arrived in England on a very cold morning in January 1961. As soon as I landed, Oh, God, I wanted to go back! What I saw I didn't believe because from the airport — it wasn't called Heathrow — it was London Airport at the time. It was a dim morning and I couldn't believe that this was the England, the Mother Country I had envisaged.

When we came off the plane, we took coaches and I came to Waterloo. Well, we were supposed to go up into a room to check out, but I didn't. I grabbed my case and saw a big gate so I went through the gate and a bloke asked, "Where are you going?"

I told him "Tottenham", so he just put me into a taxi. Years later, when I went back to change my passport, I realised that it wasn't stamped, so the woman at the embassy said, "What happened, did you stowaway to come here?" I told her, "No, I paid for my ticket and

came on a plane."
She said, "Then how come your passport isn't stamped?"
I said, "I don't know. Nobody asked me for it, nobody
stopped me, so I went my way." I didn't know I had to
clear immigration.

In London I was received by a landlady. She put me
in her sitting room to sit down. Every now and then she
would come round, take something and poke this fire
and she left. So I kept peeping at this fireplace; I wanted
to see where she would take the bread from, because I
know that at home when we baked bread we used to
poke it to check if it was ready. I couldn't see the bread,
so I asked, "Where do you take the bread from?"
She said, "That's not for making bread, that's the fire to
keep you warm."
I said, "Oh, my God."

When I was a young boy back home, I used to "warm
fire", but I never knew I would come to England to
"warm fire". Anyway, I found out that the fire was the
only heating system that they had there because when
I went up to the room that I was supposed to occupy,
I started trembling. I took this lamp and then lighted it
and I said, "Bloody hell, this is England?"

I found it very depressing when I came here to be
honest. If I could have found my fare immediately I
wouldn't be in this country now, because what I saw is
not what I expected to find.

Then I went to the Labour Exchange for a job. They signed
me on and I started moving around. I never got a job until
1st March when I got a job making carbon paper. They were
doing carbon paper and I was doing clearing up and
everything.

That first night, I went to have a bath, although the
bath was something that I scorned more or less because
what I saw in the bath I didn't want to see — there were
baby nappies, filth and everything, and then I said,

"Am I supposed to bathe in that?"
They said "Yes", so I started scouring this bath with a cleanser, you know, but although I scoured it so much, my skin was still itching because I could imagine what was in there before. But, I must have a bath now, so there was no choice. When I came out, the water was dark, so I wondered if this was the colour of the water in this country.

The following night, the same thing happened: I went to have a bath and the water was black. And when I blew my nose, something black was coming out of it, so I said uh-uh, I'm not going to do this job any more, not knowing that it was the dye from the carbon paper I was taking in, so I said, "I ain't gonna do this job no more", so I didn't go back.

The next day the landlady said, "You not going to work?"
I said, "No."
She said, "But you have to work in this country, I tell you."
I said, "But not this kind of work. I won't do it." So I refused to go back.

That Friday morning, I went down to Waterloo for a job and they gave me a job there. I used to go on the scaffolding and go and chip the wall. But, then, I couldn't take that either, and I came down and I said I don't want this because at the time you could choose a job, not like now.

Then, the following morning, I went to Manor House to London Transport for a job. I did all the preliminaries: filled in papers and then the bloke said to me, "Sorry, your application isn't successful."
I said, "Why, what happen to it?"
He said, "It's not successful."
I said all right then, so I left from there and I went down the tube and went to Griffith House, same London Transport, did the same thing and the manager said,

"All right, come back Monday morning." I'd got the job.

I stayed on the buses for years doing different jobs. Then I packed the buses up for a time and I went to the factory for a year. I went back to building for another year, and then back to London Transport.

I enjoyed London Transport, to be honest, because you were your own boss; your own guv'nor. I spent 27 years with them. I was offered driving and I turned it down; I preferred to do the conducting. When I conduct, I'm me own boss. When I'm driving, I'm everybody's boss: I'm responsible for the passengers behind me and the pedestrians on the road; everybody. And that's confinement. Conducting now, I was relaxed, you know, I could do what I wanted to do: chat up a bird, go collect a fare.

Promotion was there for me but I didn't want it. I liked things the way they were. Personally, I never found any prejudice. They called me "black" and I was proud, because, that's what I am. If they'd called me "white", I would have been upset.

One morning, on the buses, it was very cold and I sat blowing into my hands to warm up, and this woman said, "Oh, conductor, do you feel the cold?"
I said, "No, I'm made of steel."
Then she was upset and started calling me a "black bastard", but it didn't bother me.

Going to church
When I came here I wanted to go to Good Friday service, because as a young man in the West Indies I used to have to go whether I wanted to or not. So, I asked the landlady where the nearest church was and she told me, "Just go down the road and ask the vicar if you can attend church," which was strange to me, because in Jamaica I would just walk into any church once the

door was open. So, I asked the vicar and he said to me, "Personally sir, I don't mind, but I don't know what my parishioners would say."

I said, "I beg your pardon? I don't understand that."

And he said, "You see, the congregation might not want to accept you in church."

So, I said to him, "Are they God-serving people?"

He said, "Oh, yes. Oh, yes."

I said, "Then why wouldn'they accept me in the church?"

And he said, "Because you're a black person."

I said, "Then what god do they serve?"

He said, "Very good question. Sorry, I can't answer that one."

So he said, "If you want to come to church, just come in."

And I went.

There were no black-led churches at that time that I knew of, and then I heard of one in Dalston, east London, and then I started attending that until they opened up a branch in Tottenham, north London. So, church, for me, was all right; I take what I want. I wasn't a party-goer. Church was my main entertainment.

MERVIN ALEXANDER CROOKE

*Came to England from St Kitts in 1959
on a ship called The Surreyento.*

When I came to England, it was strange to me. Looking at the different atmosphere, looking at the places, it was a bit strange. I tried to look for a job and got a job eight days after I arrived.

More or less my journey started from St Kitts where I'm actually from, and slept in Barbados, took the boat the next day from Barbados and went straight to Italy. From Italy, I came across by ferry. If I can remember right, I then came straight to either Waterloo or Paddington, then made my way to an address that I was given where my uncle was living.

It's a funny thing that, coming to England. I think what made me come here was lack of associates, both girls and boys. You see, a lot of friends came before me and I began to get haunted after getting letters from them to say whether some is making good, some is making bad or what. But I was lacking companionship; thinking that I could see Tom or I could see Idris, who and me used to go along so fine and now I gotta go by the school if I want to make different friends.

Of course, I had a job at home working as a boatman, taking passengers from ships, as the ships in the harbour was out so far where you had to use boats to convey them to the dock or the pier, as they call it.

So that was my job for about three or four years, it felt all right, but as I say the companionship wasn't there no more, for after about two or three years my friends started coming here (to England). But little did I know I was jumping out the frying pan and into the fire, because two-thirds of my friends I didn't see for about, what, four or five years when I came here because the job that I got prevented me from going to where these friends were, in Birmingham, Leeds and Manchester, while I was in London.

I started working at a British Railways place in the country by the name of Cuffley. Well, telling you the truth, I had a stiff time, but my mind was made up because nobody was here to help me but me.

I started working as a porter and I took five weeks to learn the job on the station itself before I took over as a permanent guy. Then we all started to work, mucking in with each other, and, then, I was encouraged to, instead of making seven pounds a week, I could make a little more. I was instructed by a bloke who taught me the job in the station.

He said, "Listen, these leaflets that comes out every week, you could have a look at them and you will see jobs at different places on the railway that you could apply for." So, I did. Within about six months, I left Cuffley. And still being a porter, but a relief porter, which was a job that take me belly away. It meant that all relief jobs, as far as I observed, was to clean up another man's dirty work. Anyway, I did it from 1960 to 1964.

I didn't find English people extraordinary because when I left home I had a good time working for and alongside different island people, because, as I said before, I was a man who worked a boat, so that meant it carried me on steamers, yachts and everything like that, so, when I came here, it (the country and people) did not come in strange to me.

I did meet prejudice, yes, but the prejudice that I met first is when I and my uncle wanted a place to live and we were turned down about three times. They said, "No coloured, No Irish", and so on. I also met a white woman whose husband gave me the room and, when I went back to pay the money, she asked me one question, and that question was, "Where do you work?"

I said on British Rail.

She said, "Oh, no, no, no, I can't have you here, because there are people here who have to have their rest. They work 9 to 5 and you'll be coming in 4 o'clock in the mornings, 12 o'clock at nights, you'll wake them up, so I can't have you."

Anyhow, I got a flat from someone else and I lived there for about three years. It felt all right. I didn't get homesick because there was no one home for me — more or less — to be a companion with. But in a new country I felt that I would catch up with somebody.

I used to hear a lot of people say, "Oh, I'm only going to spend five years here then I'm going back home." But I never put that on myself to say that or to have that in mind.

My most memorable experience when I come to England was the different foods that I wanted to buy in the shops that I couldn't get. For instance, I once asked in a shop for a cereal that I actually liked at home, Cream of Wheat, and the shopkeeper asked me, "What's that?" I said, "Don't you know?"

She said, "Never heard of it."

I was astonished about going to buy something to eat that I was accustomed to and couldn't get. Now, that is the experience of plenty other things that West Indians asked for in certain shops, more or less Indians' or Greeks' shops, but not the English shops. Anytime you asked for anything that they hadn't got, they would write it down on a piece of paper. Next week you'd go, it's there.

BYRON LAWRENCE

Came to Britain in September 1961 from St Vincent.
He enjoyed a long career working for the Post Office.

A friend of mine received me at Shepherd's Bush, in London, which was my first place of residence. It was summer. The first thing I observed was the people in the park sunning themselves. Well, they still do that. Obviously they weren't accustomed to a lot of sun so they were making use of the little they got.

In the West Indies, we have a word: "Come see me and come live with me are two different things." In the West Indies we thought the greatest of the English people. We thought they were the greatest sportsmen.When we came, we realised that was a farce. If they don't win they're mean and nasty. When they win, the world could scarcely hold them and when they lose, they're bad losers. They're not sportsmen. I admire good sports, not any and every sport, but good sports like a good football match or a good cricket match.

I am from St. Vincent but I lived in Curaçao for 17 years before I came to England. I came to England because, at the time, lots of West Indians were coming to England.

Initially, however, I came with the intention of studying, which I did for one year. I was thinking of doing medicine so I was doing chemistry, physics and biology. I did take an exam but I only passed in chemistry, not in the others, and after one year I couldn't keep it up, so I went to work at the Post Office.

Well, as we say, there are good and bad everywhere, so you find some good people, you find some bad people, some mean people. Overall, we shouldn't have much complaint, but we know there have been difficulties and there have been misunderstandings and we have not always found things the way we would like to have found them.

I did not notice a lot personally but I know there has been a lot of prejudice. I would say I scarcely experienced any prejudice, maybe because I didn't expose myself to prejudice and, of course, we have a word back home that: "Monkey knows what tree to climb". So, you looked at a person and you'd know what you could see in that person, just from his behaviour and the way he acts or the way he speaks. You'd know the type of person he is so you'd know how to approach that person.

And we know respect demands respect. So, you're not going to shout at everybody. So, as wise as you are or as foolish as you are, you would know how to approach different people.

I am a scout leader. I associated with older people than myself. I'm a very strict person and part of my scout nature comes from spending all my life in the church. There would have been little chance of anyone taking chances with me, right? Just from the way I carried on; the way I performed. There have been little instances but nothing worthwhile talking about. But, out there, in the wide world, I could see prejudice.

I'll give you one example: some years ago, there was West Indian man, I don't know which island he was from, it could have been Dominica, and he was friendly with a white girl. There was some misunderstanding and the report is that he fired shots at the doors and windows of the house this woman was in. Just about the same time, a white man shot and killed his wife, who had a young baby. Just about the same time the two cases were tried, not at the same place, different places.

The white man who shot and killed his young wife was sentenced to three years. The black man, a West Indian, who fired shots at the house that his girlfriend was in, was sentenced to seven years. And those two things happened at the same time. There was no outcry. People saw what took place and it was just "One of those things", they would have said.

Buying houses

When West Indians came here we had no home so we had to rent a room and we had several families or several couples in a house. Just a room to each couple and one stove — one kitchen and stove for three or four families. We had to live in those conditions.

Before long, West Indians decided they had to get out of that situation, so we acquired homes. Well, that's a vast difference. Living three and four families in a house with one kitchen, one toilet and bath, and having your own home. Of course, that didn't come easily. It came as they say, "Necessity is the cause of change".

Over the years, while West Indians had acquired their own homes, you found that many of the English people had not done so. But West Indians did it though necessity.

We still know there's a lot of injustice and a lot of malpractices by the police, in particular, but people are getting to see they cannot carry on taking liberties with black people forever. We look at what is happening every now and again: a man is arrested and dies in police custody. But, of course, it doesn't happen to black men only, it happens to white men also, except it happens more, much more to black men. And we would never have a society that is perfect, but things are much better than they were when we came here, in the sense that we have worked, we have earned, we have got our homes and we can live comfortably.

Moreover, those of us who came many years ago are now pensioners and though we might not be rich, we can live on our pensions. So, that's a great change from when we came.

When we came we had to go out in the cold and the winters then were much worse than they are now. Sometimes, we left home when it was dark and returned when it was dark. Now, if you are a pensioner, you don't have to go out in the dark if you don't need to or wish to.

VICTOR ECHINWOOD

A widower, he came from Jamaica in 1960.

When I looked around, it was a different scene from in Jamaica, but the people were so polite amongst us.

Well, the weather. Phew. The first year when I came here we didn't have bad weather at Christmas, until the January. Huh! First time I see snow. I fell down about three times going to work — I said, bwoy, no way!

If I was in Jamaica and rain a-fall, I not going to work in it. But here, I have to go, yeah? So, I went to work and the place was full of staff. I said, "Bwoy, how much people work in this place?" And when I went to work I had to have my hands in my pockets to warm up. I did my job same way.

Coming out in the evening, I stand up at the bus stop, say to myself, "Bwoy, if I could find my fare, is gone I gone!" I wouldn't stay here. But, still, I coped and saw it through.

It so happen that I had to get a job and the first job that I did was at a place they called Fleetway at Bouncers Road. And I was working there over a year and my sister was working there too, so I used to try and help her out because she never worked that hard in Jamaica.

And it happened that when she left they wanted to plant me with that job too and take away the white chap and put another coloured chap — me — there. The work was spraying chairs and making tubes; they sprayed the tables and fixed them.

I worked there for a year and when the foreman came to me and said that if I don't pick them off faster he's going to give me my card. So I told him that I couldn't do the two jobs one time, so they gave me my card and I went out to the union's head office. And when I went there the rep phoned them and said, "Oh, my brother got sacked and I don't like how my brother got sacked." So, now, they got a white boy to give evidence about why they sacked me and I was out for about three months and then I went to a factory where they made stoves. That was a nice job. I liked it because it was the same thing we used to do back home. We would take the aluminium, melt it and make those little pots and things.

Finding housing

In those days, you couldn't get a council house. When you tried to get one — you just couldn't get it. When you knocked on white people's doors and them see a black man, they just closed the door.

I was going to a church. A white girl named Dot took me to church. They didn't accept me at first but, after a week, them loosened up. I did buck her up at the same workplace and I said to her, "Can I give you a letter?" She said, "Why not?"

And I went home and I wrote a letter and I gave it to her

and she gave me one back and it's there, you know, we started to mesh together. But, at the same time meshing together, I had a feeling, yeah? The fear is she's white and I'm black, and to how people — the white people them — looking at you, you feel like if the earth could really swallow you up. You know what I mean?

So, one day, I said to her, "Suppose it happen that I come and knock at your door and your father and your mother turn down on me, would you give evidence against me?" She said, "Nah, nah."

I said, "Go on, you would never speak the truth" (laughs).

You know? I tried to suss her out, until I said I can't really mesh that way, I have to send for one of my own. And I did send for one of my own. That means when we're walking I don't have no fear who wan' look and who a dis (disrespect)— I have no fear because we are all one. That's it.

But, going back, there was this guy Lucky Gordon. I knew him, and his mother used to sell all different things: cooked food and so on back home. When you wanted yankee cigarettes, don't care if any boat not in, she had yankee cigarettes.

So, when I came here and I heard that Lucky Gordon got in with Christine Keeler and all those things — I was shocked. Around that same time when I lost my job at the stove factory, a white man said to me, "Are you from the YMCA in Jamaica?"

I said, "Yes".

He said, "That's the person I'm looking for." He asked where I lived and I told him.

He said, "Can I come round to your home?" I said "Yes", but afterwards I changed my mind.

I said, "I better come to your home."

And he took me in his car. But is one intention I have, because anyhow I go a fi-him home that door is not locking (laughs).

When we got in he took off his shirt and I could see some weals across the man's back, you know? And him spin a kind of talk saying he's to get a whipping. And I whipped him — three times! Afterwards, him gimme a tenner. So I glad for this tenner, you know. So, he asked me if mi married and I said no.

Later, when my wife, Gladys, came from work, I said, "Gladys, bwoy, this is history. A man pay me a tenner to beat him (laughs)."
Mi say to her, "If you hear a car horn outside don't look because me tell the man say mi is not a married man."
So, later the man came back. And when me looked through the window, it was him. The wife said, "Victor, don't go," but I told her, "Mi well protected, man."
Mi go and mi lick (whipped) him again (laughs).

Discrimination

Prejudice was there from the '60s, but you could get jobs. You could walk out of one job and get another, you know what I mean? Everybody go off at 12 and you don't go back — you start say you feel sick and you go and look for another job.

Well, I didn't run into any Teddy Boys, but I remember one Sunday I went in a tea shop, that was about '64, and it happens there was a little coloured boy, aged about seven, when I was coming out, and three white guys had a little white guy — a little bigger than the black one — to set them to fight. So, I just stood and watched the white guy kick him, kick this little black guy.
I said, "Why you don't kick him back?"
I said, "Kick him back!"
And the little boy kicked him back since he hear me say "kick him".
I said, "Look, the three of unno stand up there who set them on to fight." If they get involved you know I must go into it, right?

So I told them, "Unno going to stand up there and see that little black boy batter that white boy."

And the little black boy put him in a neck hold till the other boy cried, "Oh, he's choking me, he's choking me!" I said, "All right, let go and come."

So we left and I just carry him go a-him yard (took him home). See, I didn't mix up in company. From back home I didn't mix up in company. I stayed away and kept to myself, but if you interfered with me, I'll do you.

Housing

In those days, too, there used to be gas wars. I would put my right money, four shillings, in the meter for the stove. The other man no put in his money but when you came down, gas and everything would be finished, so that could start a contention. We are the ones who caused those problems. We!

You see the Jew? The Jew helped lots of black people and, you know, what happened to them? Some people would get a room and nasty up the place and go to the tribunal and bring them (the inspectors) come and show them how the place stay and all that. One demanded £7000 to go. Yes, that is what they did.

DAPHNE COVER

Came from Jamaica aged 19 in 1952 with her sister,
Jenny, who was 21. Rationing was still taking place
when they arrived here.

Our mum came up before us. She had travelled *via* the United States. As a child, I had always wanted to travel and see the world, and if my mother hadn't sent for me, I probably would have become a stowaway!

We arrived on a banana boat called "The Producer" on a cold March day but we were well prepared with our coats and hats, which we had bought in Jamaica. The journey took 13 days and I was seasick all the way.

England was so gloomy. It was strange leaving behind sunshine and calypso to come and see everyone dressed in black. The windows were dark with shutters over them. People were moving so fast and they weren't friendly at all. Most places you went to, you would see signs saying, "No coloureds". If you sat next to someone on a bus and they didn't like you, they would move away. People were always looking at you as though you were something different. My poor sister cried her eyes out all the time; she wanted to go home. Not me, though, I was determined to tough it out here with the intention of going to the United States after a few years.

We were renting a place in Holloway, north London, and we had to have ration books. There was no bath in the house, we had to go to the public baths and there was a coal-fire and gaslight on the streets.

Within a week of us coming here two things happened: I became a bridesmaid — I remember taking a tram-car back from the registry office — and my sister and I both got jobs.

Before I left Jamaica, I was working as a stenographer. I had typing and shorthand skills but when I went to the Labour Exchange they said I couldn't get a job in that field, so I went to a factory repairing army uniforms. It paid £3.5.0 a week with a bonus sometimes bringing it up to £5, and we worked from eight in the morning until six at night.

I was the only black in with a sea of whites and I noticed that I would get the worse jobs to do. You couldn't prove prejudice or complain, you had to just get on with it. I felt all my hopes were dashed when I had to get a job in a factory. I was so fed up with the job and one lunchtime a friend offered to go with me to look for another one, which I got, also doing machining.

I came across prejudice in that job. There were some Greek workers who would always complain to the boss that I wasn't quick enough and they would talk about me in their own language, always using the word "Marvue" (mavro), meaning black.

Every Friday, I would leave my machine in good working order and every Monday I would come in and my machine would not work. They used to run the machine and it would get knotted up with cotton, so one weekend I took my bobbin home and I got told off. The situation got so bad that in the end I left the job.

There was another black — we said "coloured" in those days — family living nearby and at weekends we would visit them and enjoy food and music or they would visit us. Later on, people had house parties or we would go to a dance at the Lyceum in the West End or go to see a live band.

Redifussion was the main entertainment in the house because we didn't have a television, and I remember us boiling tea leaves and dyeing our tights because we couldn't get the right colour tights to buy.

In 1953, I remember watching Princess Elizabeth being crowned Queen on a little black and white television at Friend's House in north London.

In 1956, I got married. By then my mum had bought a large four-storey house with another couple and my husband and I lived there. It was good to have our own bath and electric light at last.

The younger generation now do not realise how much hardships we passed through and how much they can now take for granted.

ROBERT N. MURRAY

*Ex-serviceman from Nottingham. He came to England
from Guyana to serve in World War II.*

When, at the culmination of hostilities, (World War II), the vast majority of us either remained or returned to further our education, or to work for a short while, injustices and inhumanity really came to the fore.

The heads of gatemen, doormen and all those guardians of entrances would shake negatively as we approached in pursuit of jobs. Peepholes in offices would open and shut with alacrity just on the suspicion that we were seeking employment.

Apart from being humiliated and unmanned, I used to marvel at how accommodation — vacant one minute at the end of a telephone — would be taken the next at only a short distance away on my appearance!

In employment, bosses would blame their workers or the unions; and workers would blame unions or bosses.

In accommodation, landlords and landladies would accuse their tenants; and tenants would point the finger at their landlords or landladies. No-one would accept blame. Yet, whatever happened, we lost out.

Likewise, churches, whilst proffering their blessing, expressed the hope that we would stay away in future for the sake of the congregation, causing us to start our own places of worship. Considering that many of us had just volunteered our services in a brutal war, and were deeply patriotic, such behaviour came as a deep shock to us and was most horrible while it lasted.

It seems that one of the worst evils a person could commit was to marry across racial boundaries. When I met and married an Irish girl in the autumn of 1947, I had, indeed, committed the ultimate sin! The boycott was total — both from my family's side and my wife's.

On my side, I tried to soften the blow by informing my father (in Guyana) that I had got hitched to a "coloured" Irish lass. His reply was swift and scurrilous:
"Boy", his letter ran, "we know we're supposed to be damn stupid over here, but I ain't never heard of any blasted coloured nobody. As far as I know, them is supposed to be white people."

I was well and truly caught. Relations were severed forthwith. The same thing happened to my wife. Here we were ostracised — with only each other to cling to — when people in England started to talk about "black and white should not mix…what about the children?…and it would not last three months…and have your fun, but don't get married," and lots more.

We have survived and are still together today when all the doubters are either divorced or dead!

Mr Murray has written his memoir: Lest We Forget – The Experience of World War II West Indian Ex-service Personnel.

NORMA MACFARLANE

Came from Jamaica as a 20-year-old in 1961. She did a variety of different jobs before training as a chef and opening her own restaurant. After her son became ill, she closed the restaurant to spend more time with him and set up her own catering business.

I had left school in Jamaica the year after taking and passing the third level of examinations which were equivalent to GCSEs over here, or 'O' levels, as they used to be called. My aunt was a teacher and so I got a lot of help with my studies.

After leaving school, I had a choice of either becoming a teacher or going to secretarial school, but the opportunity also came up for me to come to England, so that's what I did.

My friends were travelling to England and other places, so that gave me the incentive to go as well. By then, I had a one-year-old daughter whom I left with my grandmother, who had also raised me. That part was hard but

I didn't want to turn down the opportunity. My grand-mother didn't want me to go but my mind was set. My father had been in England during the war and I had un-cles that I was coming to, so I had some idea of what to ex-pect but, to tell you the truth, I was really surprised when I came and saw the buildings all looking so much like factories.

I came with the intention of furthering my education, so, foremost in my mind was signing up at college. My uncles wanted me to join the WRENs (Women's Royal Naval Service) , but I don't think I was cut out for any-thing like that. I went to do evening classes in English history, shorthand and typing, and I also got a job on the production line at Heinz food factory. I didn't like working in that factory and only stayed for two months.

I then got an office job with a firm of booksellers and publishers which I kept for 15 years. My next position was as a clerk-typist and the company trained me to use computers when they first began to come in during the 1970s. The only reason that I left that job was because the company closed down. Not only did I not have any problems in the workplace, but I, the only black, was made supervisor of 15 girls. That job was given to me by a South African and I was surprised at how well he treated me, given that he was a white South African.

I got married in 1962, a year after coming here. I was fortunate that I didn't go through the experience of rent-ing rooms because all three of my uncles had houses of their own and one uncle bought another house just to rent. When I got married we lived in that house and I was responsible for the lettings. My uncle told me not to let to anyone with children but I thought that was too hard so occasionally, behind his back, I would rent out a room to someone with kids.

In those days, it was hard to get somewhere to rent if you had children or if you were in a mixed race relationship. Personally, I didn't really have any experience of racism but I heard about what was happening in Notting Hill, where many black people were being beaten up.

Entertainment back then was mainly house parties, but I had had a strict upbringing and, because I was living with my uncles, it was like a home from home, so I wasn't able to go out as much as most young people my age. At nine o'clock I would get told to get in the house, even though my white friends nearby were able to stay out until much later. I didn't rebel, though, because I didn't want a bad report to go back to my grandmother because that would have hurt her; something I never wanted to do.

I went back to Jamaica in 1975 to visit my sick father and my grandmother. She was an incredible lady, a woman and ten men rolled into one. She ran a successful business and was responsible for employing a large number of people. She made a big impression and has always been an inspiration.

In England, I can only remember one black business, a man called "Mi Amigo", who used to travel from house to house selling black cosmetics because, back then, you couldn't get make-up for black people in the shops. I was motivated to go into business and set up my own restaurant because I saw my grandmother run her own business very successfully and also because I have never wanted to work until I was 60. My aim was to build up the clientele of the business, put it into profit and then sell it off, but my son developed MS and I didn't want to put him into a care home so I closed the restaurant so that I could take care of him.

All in all, the experience of coming to England has been fulfilling and I think the opportunity was there for all of us who came to make our contribution and to make something of ourselves and our community.

MATHILDA LEWIS

*Aged 19 when she came from Aruba in 1959. She later
went back to the Caribbean for a short time before going on
to settle in the United States. She returned to live in Britain
in the late 1990s and set up her own charity.*

It was summer and I remember I was wearing a
summer dress that my aunt had made. My mum and
dad were already here since the early '50s and I came
to join them.

It was scary travelling on my own, especially with
all those sailors making vulgar remarks to some of the
women, but I spent a lot of the time in my cabin keeping
myself to myself. The journey took about three weeks
and finally we arrived in England. I can remember taking the train to Waterloo.

My first impression was of how all the houses looked
alike. It wasn't too long after the war and we were living in an old house in the east end of London which had
been abandoned during the war.

I clearly remember travelling with my sister on the tube and there were some elderly white people who cried out, "Look, Jamaicans, run!" And they took off. We were no danger to them but they acted so strangely. We felt bad.

English people were not very nice at that time towards foreigners. They would nudge and elbow us out of the way whenever we were walking down the street and tried to make it look like an accident, but it wasn't. We got a lot of knocks from them.

They were very superstitious of black things, like black cats or Friday 13th or black people, which were supposed to be unlucky. The Irish had their own problems too, because English people didn't like them either.

Soon after I came, my mum bought a house from some Jewish people on the same road that we were living on. All the houses have since been condemned. I know because I went back some time ago and was shocked to see that my road no longer existed. That made me quite sad.

I remember going to look for a job and on that day I set off to go to Whitechapel. Well, I arrived at a lovely place which made me think I was living in a slum; the place was so nice. I said to the lady, "Am I still in England?" She replied, "Look around you, this is London Bridge." I said, "I know a song about London Bridge", and straight away I started singing, "London Bridge is falling down". I was so happy. It was a song we had learned back home in Aruba and I was excited to be at that place in the song, London Bridge. Afterwards, I had to try and work out how to get home.

I asked a gentleman who was passing and he gave me directions for how to get back on the tube. I followed the instructions and arrived home safely, but when I told my mother that I had gone to London Bridge, all she could say was, "Here you go again with your stories." She did not believe me.

Eventually, I did get a job working in a jewellery factory for two Jewish men, Freeman and Vicmire, making lovely jewellery. I was making £5 a week for working from 8am to 6pm.

I met my husband on the job. He was from Trinidad and after we married I had three children, one after the other and I was only 23. It was hard for us trying to live in this country, finding somewhere to live which would accept children and so on, so I took the children and went to my husband's family in Trinidad.

On the boat out, there were some other people also escaping England. One woman was singing, she was so happy, but, sad to say, she suffered a mental breakdown on the trip.

Eventually, after living in the Caribbean, I went to the United States and married again, making a much better life for myself because opportunities are much better there than in England. But, I decided to return to London in the 1990s because I feel there is something I have to do which is to gather our Caribbean women together to share our stories and experiences, because we are truly heroes. Look at all the things that we have done: working so hard, taking care of the children, making ends meet and all the other problems we have overcome. Those conditions were truly horrible. We had to share toilets, do our cooking on the landing and there was so much trouble trying to find somewhere decent to live. We need to write it all down and make sure that the children today know about our struggles and our stories.

I was away from England for more than 30 years but when I came back for a holiday I felt so encouraged by the positive things that have taken place over the years, and I wanted to come and play my part. I am involved in community work now and my aim is to try and get involved in projects which will make a difference, especially for the youth, because they are the future.

MICHELLE CHARLERY

From St Lucia, she came to Britain in 1959, aged 16.

The weather was very bad, very foggy. I think the name of the boat was "The Britainnia". We spent about fourteen or fifteen days on the sea and then when we arrived at Southampton, we took the train to London Bridge or Waterloo.

I thought England would be a beautiful place, like a palace, let's put it that way, but while I was on the train I was looking around and I saw a lot of houses with chimney tops sending out smoke — at that time chimneys were more frequently used than they are now, because people burned coal. And, I saw some sheep, horses and cows in the field. It was all so different to how I had imagined.

I was wearing a suit my mum had made for me. It was very stylish and fashionable and I had a scarf or a hat she'd given me to wear with it. It was too light for the cold weather, and when I came they had to get me a coat, a cardigan and things like that and they told me

I must keep myself warm with a scarf around my neck, my coat and everything. It was all a bit of a shock. I thought the streets would be like back home streets, but we didn't have traffic lights at the time and here you had to look left and right before you crossed the road. It was so busy and I found it a bit strange. But, eventually, I did get to know places and had people telling me where to go and to always mark the name of the road where I am going and when I'm coming back.

Then, I was living near Hackney Hospital and I got a little job in a handbag factory where I used to do stapling. I was there for a while but things were hard, living in one room. It was easy at the time to get work, though, but at some places they used to say "No coloureds".

Anyway, I got a job in a bag factory and I worked there for a while and then I left. I also worked in a clothes factory and I worked there for a while and then I left. I also worked in a clothes factory doing hemming and did quite a few other jobs, including working in typewriter factory, as well.

We were working for less money at the time, but things were very cheap, because we used to go to the shops with ten pounds or ten shillings, whatever we called it, and we could buy all our bits and pieces: chicken, milk, sugar, rice and flour on top of that for the whole week. We used to survive, let's put it that way.

The house I lived in was three storeys, one of those big old buildings and I was on the middle floor. The cooker was on the landing. They didn't have a bathroom, we had to go to the public bath. That was a new experience for me but it was ok. It was just like you'd go to a swimming pool, but there was no swimming pool. Instead, everybody had their indivi-dual shower. You would go there with everything: your soap, towel, and every Saturday we used to have a bath, while in the week, what we'd do was wash top and tails, let's put it that way, and use a bowl to wash our feet.

When I left that address I went to live somewhere where there was a bath, and everybody had to share because it was only the one bath in the house. I stayed there a good while then I got pregnant with my second child, a boy.

Eventually, I had to leave that house because it wasn't convenient for kids. I had to go and get a bigger place. In those days, when you had the children it was just like being in prison, because it was only one room. When they wanted to play you had to take them to the park. If the children were running in the house the landlord or landlady would say, "The children are making too much noise." So, you just had to tell them, "Shhh! Don't make any noise."

It was hard at that time, not like now. Some houses didn't allow you to have children so I'd have to leave and try another place, so it difficult was for me at that time. I didn't have anybody to help me wash and things. that was the hardest time for me because you know when you have a new-born baby and your parents are not there you have to get on and do your own thing.

That was a bit hard for me. A lot of people have their parents here with them when they're having children now. They find themselves lucky, very lucky, but I wasn't. I found that I was a bit tearful a lot the time and the child's father didn't bother about me although I had known him for a long time before the baby came, but he didn't bother and that was hard.

From one house to another I started to buy things and pack them up in boxes. As I moved around, some things got broken here and there. It was hard, you know, when you are on your own, but you tried your best. You're working to earn your money, you have to send some money back home because, obviously, you had to pay your family back the money they'd spent on your fare to come here. And, then you had to buy yourself new clothing because you came here in what you were wearing when you left home and they were not right for the climate.

Besides, you needed a set for work and one for when you were going out; a thick coat, stockings to keep you warm, winter boots, things like that. It was especially hard when you were alone and at that time you didn't know where all your friends were, so you had to try and think for yourself.

Friendships

When we would go to the blues dances we got to meet one or two new friends, then we would keep in touch and get to know them. That was the part that kept you going because I am not overdoing it when I say it was hard, very hard.

If I had my time over and over again would I still come? Yes, because if you were not shy to meet and talk to people and to have a go at making a better life for yourself, you could get away with it. That's how I look at it.

I wanted to show my family that encouraged me to come that I could make something of myself and give my children a chance, and I did do that, so it was not in vain.

My parents said it would be better for me to come over here and everybody was coming to England so they thought they would send me to see what England looked like and I had to to try to get a better job to make something of myself.

Things are more open now, much brighter. Britain is more developed and English people are a lot better now because now they will they will talk to you, before they wouldn't. Not even in the bus did they want to sit beside you; a long time ago they wouldn't. They would stand up there, they wouldn't sit beside a black person but now they will even start a conversation.

I can remember sometime in the sixties, I was going along the street and I saw an old lady trying to tip-toe to walk across the road so I grabbed her hand and said, "Come on, love, I'll help you cross over."
She shouted, "Let go of my hand, you bloody bastard! I don't want you to touch me!"
So, I told her I was only trying to help her but, anyway, I let her carry on whatever she was doing. You used to get a lot of abuse a long time ago; they didn't want to touch you, they didn't want to sit beside you. From you were black they didn't want to know, but now things are completely different.

TOM MORGAN

He was born in Montserrat and travelled to England from Barbados in April 1957 on an Italian boat which stopped off at Tenerife and Genoa en route.

Since it was night it wasn't possible to see the famous White Cliffs of Dover, as we came into the dock at Dover. From there we took a train to Waterloo and as the train was going along you could just see people huddling up against one another, practically sitting on top of each other trying to keep warm.

It was the first time that I was seeing snow and I had never experienced cold like that in my life. I tell you, it was extremely cold. I had some jumpers but nothing prepared me for that kind of thing.

As we were travelling along, I could see the smoke coming from buildings and it put me in mind of the oil refineries in Curaçao where I had been working for ten years soon after leaving the army. My first thought was that there were a lot of factories and industries in this country. At first I didn't realise the smoke was coming form people burning coal in their houses.

What had made me come in the first place? In the army I was a regimental signaller and had travelled all over the Caribbean. When I demobbed, I decided to go back home and shortly afterwards was offered work in Curaçao, where I was a foreman.

After ten years, the contract finished and I went back home but found I couldn't get a job in Montserrat, not even a government job, so I went to Barbados to do business with a fellow I knew from Curaçao but that didn't work out, so rather than go back to Montserrat I decided to come to England.

I had a nephew here and it was he whom I came to. Well, the first impression wasn't good. My nephew and I had to share one room and it was most embarrassing. Soon after I came the landlord asked me if I wanted a job and I asked him, "doing what?"

He said as a labourer and I turned him down, although my nephew took the job. I had had some training in carpentry from back home and so I decided that was what I would do.

I got my first job with William Press and Sons at Willoughby Lane in Tottenham, north London. The shop was fully equipped and I got all my training on the job. When north sea oil production started, the company got a big contract and I found myself travelling all over the country, from Scotland to Dorset, working on different jobs and on different sites.

I used to play cricket — that was one of my passions from back home. As the only coloured player in the works team I had made a big impression as a batsman and bowler. I was the best bowler they had up to when I left the company and they even used to send and ask me to come and play for them after I'd left the job.

Anyway, the governor of the firm — we knew him as "Mr

All Press" (I don't know his name apart from that) — owned a farm in Surrey and every summer a works team from Tottenham would go and play a team in Surrey.

Well, the captain didn't want to take me along because I was coloured but the rest of the team kicked up a stink and said that I was their best bowler, so they couldn't leave me out. Next thing I knew, a car was sent to take me and my wife to the farm in Surrey.

To my surprise, the governor was waiting to greet us and took us into the marquee and sat with us at table talking about the match that was coming up and everything. I was so pleased by all this that I told him, "I am going to win you the match today." And I did. I bowled out all the other team and scored a heap of runs so that my team mates lifted me on their shoulders and marched me around the grounds singing.

The governor was very happy that we'd won. He came up to me afterwards and asked me if I was happy with where I was living. I didn't want to create any problems so I told him yes, even though that wasn't true.

Later on, back on the job, one of the fellows told me that I should have said no because he would have offered me one of the company's houses. I didn't know and it was too late to go back on what I had said. Sadly, a couple of years later the governor died while working on a contract in Nigeria. I went to his memorial service at one of the cathedrals in London.

I left the job about two or three years after that because there was a foreman there who didn't get along with anybody and he kept making things hard for me, putting off the jobs that should have come to me and in the end I just got my cards and went on to a job at Hackney borough, and stayed there for five years before going on to do agency work as self-employed. I was promoted to foreman and did that until I retired in 1989.

Finding housing

When I first came, it was difficult living in just one room, so I got in touch with a housing agency in Dalston, east London. I think it was called, Donaldsons, and I spoke to them on the phone about renting a flat. They told me to come along to their offices but when I went, the clerk at the desk asked me what I wanted. I told him I was Mr Morgan who rang them up and he said, "Sorry, Mr Morgan, we don't deal with coloureds."

I was so angry and frustrated that I decided the best thing was to get my own place. I had a house in Montserrat at the time so I decided to sell it and buy a place here. I bought my first house at 22 Grove Road, Tottenham, for £2,500.

In those days you could get houses for £900. The reason I sold the place was because it was prone to flooding. One time it rained very heavily so that we were using large brooms to sweep the water out of the workplace, but when I went home the whole of my house was flooded. They had to rip up the floorboards and lay a new one. I decided it could happen again so I sold up. The next place I bought was in 1966 and I am still living there now.

What about parties?

Parties, yea man! Every Saturday night there were house parties. And the thing was, you only had ginger wine in those days — Stones Ginger Wine — or else Ruby wine, and the ginger wine would give you such a headache! The morning after the party your head would feel like it was coming off. If you saw someone holding their head, you knew they had been drinking that ginger wine.

There were parties all over but I wasn't too much into them, except for the birthday parties and such that I was invited to, because all you were getting most of the time was watered down drinks.

Plus, they charged too much for you to go in and too much for the drinks, so most of the time it was a fiasco. But, this one time, a fellow came for me to go to a house party with him and I never wanted to go. He kept on and on. I went there but I refused to go in. I just didn't want to know and waited outside.

Anyway, he came out and offered to give me a lift home and I remember us stopping at a traffic light and then the car spinning out of control and crashing. I was thrown from the front to the back and kept passing out and coming back round and the next thing I knew I was in the Prince of Wales Hospital.

I was in a lot of pain, my face was swollen and bloody and I had fractures. The doctors thought my ear-drums were damaged and needed operating on, but it turned out not to be that serious, although I now have hearing problems, which I think was caused by that accident. All in all, I was lucky to be alive but the fellow who had been driving never came into that ward to see me or even said sorry. After that, I finished with house parties. They weren't all they were cracked up to be.

Going back home

If I had my time again, I would not have come to England, I would have stayed in Montserrat. The conditions here were not like we had heard about and the treatment was not what we had expected. Even in the army we were promised this and that but none of it materialised and when we came here we found something different to what we had been told.

Now, I can't go back to Montserrat because of the volcano, but if I did go back to the West Indies it would be to Antigua, because I went there in the army and liked it, and I have some relatives there. But, really, it is too late now to be thinking of going back to live. I have grown up children and they are still depending on me.

TOM GREENAWAY

From Montserrat, he came to England in 1954 and worked as an engineer. A fine balladeer, he performed in pubs and clubs up and down the country. He still enjoys singing and playing cricket in his spare time.

When I came here I didn't intend to stay; it was just for a couple of years but when I catch myself, I was loaded down too much in the country so I didn't try to go back home, I just decided to stay on.

It was very hard; very tough. We used to have the Teddy Boys, the leather jackets, everybody against us but we fight it over. We tried to get on top of them so till, in the end, they came to be friends with us because they were scared of us.

We opened the way for a lot of people to come here in the sixties because if we weren't tough we would have gone back home. Instead, we opened the way for those who came later on.

My first wage was £4.50 a week, which was about one-and-sixpence an hour. That was good money in those days, and you had three people living in one room paying a pound each, but we survived. I was working in engineering and I stayed in that same job for 27 years as a charge hand and then part-foreman.

At the end of the day, times were hard in the eighties and we only had a two-day week and since I had a family of six kids, I couldn't manage so I asked for voluntary redundancy.

We in this country couldn't give up; we had to go to the people and find their way, understand their mind and attitude. I don't walk away from people, I go to them and when I went to them they came to me. Right now, I'm very respected in this country. I'm happy now.

Finding a place to live was very hard: they didn't want kids, they didn't want blacks or Irish; you had to be lucky to get a place. I lived in a hostel when I first came. I had been living in the United States for four years so I knew about living in a big city and I could fend for myself and fend for others, too. I looked after them, took them to the doctor, the dentist, or to look for a job and, since I used to work nights, I hardly used to get any sleep.

It was only one room but sometimes four or five people would come and I'd put them up, take care of them, go to work, buy food for them to cook. They didn't need to pay me because these were my own people and I would take care of them until they got their own place.

In the 1950s, you could get a house for £2-3,000 and now it's worth £350,000, but, because I didn't intend to stay, I didn't buy a house until much later, although my cousin and my brother-in-law bought houses.

When I came, I found the society hard but it made me very hard as well and I was able to show other people the way to get on.

I taught my kids the way to get on in life; how to stay out of trouble. I have six daughters and when they were growing up I told them that unless they were 18 they couldn't bring any boyfriend into my house. Once they were 18, they could bring whoever they liked because they were old enough to stand on their own and they all did what I told them and, today, they have all got on well in life. They work in good jobs: in banks, insurance, jobs like that, and one is a journalist. They are all in the United States. I go there for holidays but I tell people that this (Britain) is the best country in the world.

Entertainment

As far as entertainment went in the old days, I used to entertain myself and entertain other people singing in clubs and pubs and bingo halls and at Christmas parties, that sort of thing. I won a lot of singing and dancing competitions because I used to do ballroom dancing, the foxtrot; you name it, and then I used to sing and play the guitar. The songs I did were mainly ballads; songs to make your heart feel sad; songs like, *For the Good Times*, or *Moon River*, and *Promise Me, Darling*.

I had an opportunity to cut records but through neglectfulness I didn't get to do it. I even went to the BBC and they gave me a guitar to play and forms to fill out, but I never bothered with it. I just stuck to pubs and clubs, weddings and christenings; anything people wanted me to do, I would do. I'm not bashful; I'm full of pluck and I have a high mind, so I get along good with anybody.

KEN CORBIN

A former carpenter who went on to work as a bus driver. He arrived in England from Barbados in June 1956.

The first impression was very lousy because I saw the smoke coming from the chimneys and I thought, "What a lot of baker shops!" It was far from what I had expected it to be.

The living conditions were very poor as well for a big country; people had outdoor toilets and, as far as the bathing situation, people had to go to public baths and pay five pence — today's equivalent of a shilling — or six pence, and stand in a queue to wait for your turn to take a bath. You'd say how you wanted it, hot or medium, or whatever. It was not very good.

Most of us who came to this country came to work for five years and, we thought we could go back home, set ourselves up, but it was not that easy. That's what drove a lot of us to buy our own houses at the end of the day, because the living conditions were very poor:

living in one room and not being allowed visitors after seven o'clock, all the rest of it. It was lousy, as I said. Before I came, I had heard such fancy stories about this country. It was just a dream, really, but when I came and saw white men shovelling coal or sweeping the streets and so on — and they looked black because they were so dirty — it was something different altogether.

And there were some dirty people around. They've tidied themselves up since West Indians came here because, when I was a carpenter, I would see someone drink from a cup on Friday and on Monday morning he would take that same dirty cup and pour tea and drink from it. And many of them used to condemn the black women for their bright colours and now look: it's all transformed; everybody's wearing these colours.

What caused the problems is that in the West Indies we were taught a lot about the English but the English people knew little or nothing about us. Once we were black they would ask you which part of Africa or which part of Jamaica you came from; those were the two countries they knew at the time. That's the way it was.

Work was very easy to find back then and even housing because if you had problems with your landlord you could go and find something else. I don't know how people manage today paying £70 a week for childcare. I paid £2 for one child and I can't see how people do it now, especially if they want to buy a place; that is almost impossible.

In the winter we used to burn paraffin heaters and put the kettle on top to boil so that in the morning we could get some warm water to wash with. Nowadays, people take heating and hot water, all these facilities, for granted.

Well, I had a couple of tiffs with Teddy Boys, nothing big but I always learned to defend myself and I had to bash a couple of them up to be honest with you. I had a few friends who got chased with bicycle chains over Ladbroke Grove side. And I had a cousin who went to Piccadilly, which we all used to do, visiting the Piccadilly highlight spots on a Sunday night, but this particular time someone took a swing at him. My cousin was a big, strong man and he gave the bloke one punch – he went up in the air and dropped on the ground. That was it, fight finished.

Times have really changed because today you can hire a hall or a club to put on a dance but we only had blues parties where you invited people to the house and had a nice party. You would prepare your chicken, souse, and patties to sell and some people would contribute two or three pounds to prepare everything. So, people would come to dance and enjoy themselves. That was our entertainment.

Clubs? No, although I myself used to go to the Astoria in Tottenham Court Road, in central London, to do ballroom dancing, jive, the waltz, foxtrot and the quickstep; all that. It was very entertaining, but otherwise it was mostly a house to house thing; going from one part of London to another to do our boogie.

Equal pay is something that I was really grateful for because when I came I was doing carpentry work and when I finished with that I went to do car renovation. You would be working next to a white man doing a better job than him and getting less wages, but the law changed that and brought in equal pay, so that was very good.

I chucked in the car renovation and thought to myself, "these are the days of cheap labour", and I didn't want to give my labour to just one person so I took a day off and went to Ford Motor Company, which was one of the best paying employers at the time, and did some work for them. Then I took a job with London Transport as a bus driver, which I did for 24 years and eight months.

I didn't think about retiring in this country because

I never planned to stay but, now, I'm OK with it; it's not so bad. White people don't pass you and not say "Hello" nowadays. For me, I would say they're a bit more civilised now.

MR BEN

*Mr Ben came to England from Jamaica in 1959
and did a variety of different jobs before retiring.*

I came here to work and to try and better myself. I know a lot of people say it, but I really did have a plan to come and stay for just five years, that's all, but the five years never came and I am still here.

Before coming to England, I had gone to the United States to do farm work. That was in my 20s when I got a contract to go and work in Florida where we were mainly picking oranges and grapefruits, that sort of thing. It was hard work and you had to be fit to manage the workload, but I was young and in the peak of health so that was no problem for me.

I did that for six months and it was quite good. When we weren't working we got to see some of the state, especially in Tampa, Florida, and we got to have some good times off the job. I always say that if I did get the chance I would have tried to stay, but I was silly. I should have found a girl and tried to settle down with her and get my stay but I didn't do that and when the contract finished I went back to Jamaica.

I stayed there for a little while but I couldn't settle; I had the travel bug and I wanted to go and see what England was like and if I could get some work and the chance to try and progress in life.

In those days it was easy to go to England. A lot of our people were travelling there because they believed it was a good place to be and that there would be a lot of opportunities for jobs and so on. All you needed was for someone to sponsor you with somewhere to live until you could work your way up and find your own place.

It so happened that I didn't have anyone in England to sponsor me, but a friend of mine was going over there and she said I could stop with her until I found somewhere for myself and that's what I did. We travelled together and I lodged with her family for six months until I got my own room and started up from there.

The first thing there was to notice about England was how cold it was. In those days it was very cold, not like now when the winters are not too bad. And, on top of that, it was very difficult to get a room. You either had to rely on those black people who came and bought a house or you took your chances, but there was a lot happening to put you off because white landlords didn't like to rent their place to blacks.

Also, if you did get a place, you had a lot of rules and regulations about what you could or couldn't do. For instance, you couldn't come in after nine o'clock. They were very strict. I couldn't afford a flat and, back then, the living conditions were very poor: you had to live and cook and do everything in the same little room and that created problems. I'm not a trade person but I was prepared to settle for anything; any kind of work to earn some quick money and that's what I did.

It was easy to find work. You could just move from job to job and if you were in a job paying six pounds and another job was going across the road paying seven pounds, for that one extra pound you would leave your job and take it because that one extra pound could go a long way. You could do a lot of shopping and pay your rent, which for me was about two-and-six in the old money, and I could save up maybe a pound a week.

When I came to England, I was homesick for about two or three weeks but after that I was OK. I decided to save up and send for my sister, which I did after about a year. I wanted to give her a chance because things were really hard out in Jamaica, so I saved up and eventually sent for her.

It was easy to make friends with the English people. I used to work with them in the factories and sometimes I was the only black person in the workplace, so you had to try your best to get along with everyone. If anything, I found them quite helpful. I wasn't the kind to get into trouble and I didn't really come across any trouble with the teddy boys and so on, although I know some people had problems in areas like Notting Hill. Later on, I went to work over there and found it all right. Nobody really troubled me and I am not the sort to get into arguments or fights. Anyway, People were more friendly in those days.

For entertainment we always used to have our house parties and there were a few clubs around the place run by black people. In the '60s I remember one in Mile End, in the east end of London and another one across town in Paddington, west London, where we would go and dance to blue beat and ska. As far as the music, Prince Buster was the main man and he had some good tunes at the time, hits like *Al Capone, Madness, and Enjoy Yourself.*

Sometimes people used to have house parties where they would put out all their furniture and hold a dance in their place. We would have a good time but sometimes the police would come and mash it up, take away the drinks and the curry goat; everything.

I remember one time we were at a party and this white lady came in. She wasn't with anyone, she was just by herself and she bought a drink and started dancing and enjoying herself along with us. It turned out that she was a plain clothes undercover police officer, but we didn't know.

Anyway, after a while she left and then came back with a group of uniformed police and they broke up the dance and started looking for drugs. Later on we found out that the police woman had marked the money she used to buy her drink. That's how they used to do it in those days. I think they arrested the guy whose party it was because he was selling drinks without a licence. But, for all that, we still used to look forward to the weekend and the chance to go out and enjoy ourselves.

I started helping out with a few sound systems and then began my own one as a hobby in the early 1970s. Music is my first love and that will never change.

PHYLLIS KNIGHT

Phyllis came to England on sabbatical from her job in 1957, when she was in her mid-20s. It wasn't long before opportunity knocked and she was on the move again, but she eventually settled in London.

I didn't come to stay or to look for work. In fact, I didn't emigrate. I came here because, in those days, if you were a civil servant (as I was in Trinidad), you got the same things as the white civil servants who were from overseas. I had three months' leave from my job and my passage paid to go to England, which was my entitlement.

So, I came to London and — once I got here — what a revelation! I came in May, during a beautiful summer, and I loved it straight away. I looked around and there was culture on every side you looked. There were things going on at the Royal Court theatre and, oh, my goodness, I fell in love with London; the place was literally buzzing.

A lot of the people who were economic migrants were the ones who probably had the hardest time because they came and had no job and nowhere to live. It is important to remember that those pressures were not really on me, so I was fortunate in that regard.

I came here on my own, but there were one or two people up here that I knew: one of my elder sisters, Sheila, who was married to the playwright and actor Errol John, was living in Ealing, and Pearl Prescod, the singer and actress who was a family friend from back home, was also up here. Although we were not blood relations, our families were very close. Her son, Colin Prescod, (the academic and activist) was born in our home in Trinidad. I've known him since he was just a baby and I've got some pictures of him sitting on my lap.

His mother was very interesting and talented performer. Before she had left, there was a music festival in Trinidad and Pearl had the most exquisite singing (and speaking) voice and she sang *Danny Boy*. An influential music teacher, May Johnstone, who was in the audience, heard her and after Pearl had finished singing, May ran to the back of the stage and held on to Pearl and told her, "I have never heard a voice like that. You must have a scholarship!" And she arranged for Pearl to go to England and do her musical training. She ended up acting and touring Europe with Katherine Dunham, the celebrated dancer, and had a career in British film and television.

The 1950s were an interesting and exciting period for many reasons, including the fact that countries were getting their independence and white colonial rule was being replaced, like Ghana, which had become independent in 1957.

In London, I had the chance to interact with students from all over the world. The British Council had a place in central London, and we also used to lime (hang out) at the Student Centre in Earl's Court. That was the famous meeting place for young West Indians and Africans in those days.

Anyway, at that time (in 1957), Marcus Garvey's first wife, Amy Ashwood Garvey, had set up a boarding house at 1 Bassett Road called the Afro People's Centre, I think, just near Labroke Grove tube station. So, Ma Garvey, as we called her, was a leading light and we ended up eventually renting rooms at her centre.

Ma Garvey was writing her autobiography around that time and I used to help her with some typing, although I don't know what happened to the book.

In the summer of 1958, my father came up here because my brother had been studying medicine in England and Daddy came up for his graduation. Colin Prescod, Pearl's son, also arrived that summer. By now his mum and I had got a little flat and that was to be his home.

When he came, he was attending an excellent school in Notting Hill called Holland Park School. The Labour MP, Tony Benn, had a son who was also going to that school, as was Polly Toynbee, the journalist.

I remember one evening when I came home from work (as a typist), there was Colin by himself sitting facing the bay window. The child was frozen on the spot in front of that window, deep in thought. What happened was that he had just walked down the road and outside our fence somebody had written some graffiti saying, "Big Wog", which we suspected was directed at his mother.

Imagine, this child coming to England and this was his first experience of London. That was the summer of 1958, the same year that the Notting Hill riot riots broke out.

You know, some things are hard to reconcile. I mean, I have a lot of British friends myself, my sister married an Englishman, and my brother married an English girl, but when things like that happened, you asked yourself searching questions about the attitude of the British, you know?

At that time there was a medical student up here, a boy called Richie Haynes, who was from Trinidad. He got caught right at the corner of Ladbroke Grove tube station just when they were rioting. And he backed up against a wall and just then he saw a policeman and he called him to help but the policeman said, "No, no, no. If I do anything for you they're going to cap (kill) me, so you better find your own way and get to where you're going."

That was the temperature in Notting Hill Gate in the summer of 1958. And, I mean, I don't want to be like James Baldwin when he says you don't want to say that all white people are bad, but you know that whole thing makes you think...

Eventually, we got in with a group of young West Africans who said to me, "They are 'Nigerising' (promoting Nigeria's independence) now, the whites are leaving the country, so wouldn't you like to go and get yourself a job in Nigeria?"

I said, "Why not?", but I didn't really take the application or the idea of going there seriously. But would you believe, I got the job! That just shows you that you should never generalise because you never know how things could work out.

Here was I: I was black, I was female, I was trained and do you know that those three things, which are normally considered liabilities, were assets for me getting that job in Nigeria as a professional librarian? That is what I was already doing as a civil servant back home where I was in charge of the public library in San Fernando.

Notice the dates: I arrived here in May 1957 and did not leave until October 1958, so I was here for more than a year before leaving to go to Africa. At that time,

Nigeria was divided into three regions under a tripartite system: northern, western and eastern regions. Remember, we're talking about more than 50 years ago, and we had students from all the different ethnic tribes, there were no ethnic conflicts.

Do you know, there are still people who have known me all my life who still hold it against me that I went to work in Nigeria? They asked me, "What on earth did you think you were doing?" When I went back to Trinidad there were people who were annoyed that I had gone to Africa. I suppose they thought it was a rather odd thing to do and to them it was scandalous that I had chosen to go to Africa when I could have settled in England. They considered Africa backward and inferior and their attitude was, *"Why would you want to go there?"*.

That is how prejudiced and colonial-minded some of us were and still are. They held it against me because I actually embraced the chance to go to the continent. But, those three years from 1958 until 1961 that I spent in Africa were the time of my life.

Some people went to West Africa to "find their roots", but I didn't go to find roots, I went because I got a job there. An English man was my boss in the north of Nigeria, but then I was transferred to the south where I headed up the library in Ibadan.

I remember jet planes were new then, and as I flew in and looked down at Africa for the first time — I can't find words to describe how I felt and the effect that had on me; it was a life-transforming experience.

In the Caribbean, before Eric Williams, we had never had intellectual leaders who were black. Yet, in Africa we had a whole set of intellectuals who were black and did not devalue themselves the way some black Trinidadians and black West Indians did. This was their land, they were Africans in Africa, and their mindset — especially the ones who had gone to college — was different. I was seeing my identity and myself in a whole new way.

It is hard to explain the difference I felt as a young West Indian girl living and working in Nigeria, and living and working in the West Indies. There was such a sense of belonging that I have not had anywhere else, and I knew from my time in London that England was not going to give me the same sense of belonging. Working in Nigeria was a tremendous experience for me; I haven't the words to describe it.

For example, I remember going into a chapel in Ibadan and seeing a fantastic sculpture in ebony called *The Risen Christ* by Ben Enwonwu, a young Nigerian sculptor, and I stood there and just looked at this amazing object. I had never seen a more beautiful sculpture in my life.

Anyway, after my contact expired, I returned to England from Nigeria, but it wasn't long before I was off back to Trinidad again for a brief visit. After that, the opportunity came for me to go and study at the University of the West Indies in Jamaica from 1961 to 1964. Then, in 1964 I returned to England.

At that time they had introduced immigration restrictions and many colonials were denied access, but I swept in on a spanking new British passport, which had been renewed for me before I'd left Nigeria.

In London, I worked briefly at the London County Council (LCC) as an education librarian. When I think of what I had been doing in Nigeria, it made me realise that I wasn't moving forward very much; I was standing still. You have to remember that I grew up in a house where there were expectations that we could really achieve and my parents and siblings were high-fliers.

When I came up here I found that the people who qualified as librarians were not intellectuals, unlike in Trinidad, and to be honest I did not find the job very inspiring.

The only inspiring job that I held in Britain came years later when Ken Livingstone became the head of the Greater London Council (GLC, formerly the LCC) and was dishing out money for community development.

I joined a training project called the Caribbean Communications Project. One of the project's roles was to teach literacy to mature students. While working there, I did some studying and got a diploma to teach literacy. I worked with that project until 1985 when it closed, and that was the end of my working life, really.

All in all, my experience in England started well but ended badly, because once an unhappy love affair left me clinically depressed. People looked at me and said that I made some wrong decisions about my relationships and my career decisions, but I didn't agree with them.

Unfortunately, there was a lot of pressure to live up to other people's expectations. The depression held me back because, without it, I might have achieved more. However, a turning point came when I went back into studying and what my tutors did for me was to release me to be myself again. Up to that point I had felt like I was a cork that was being held under water. It will stay there as long as it is held down, but if someone comes along and releases that cork, it will float up.

That's what they did for me: they allowed me to float back up to the surface and that experience of going back into education, surrounded by young people, has been a tremendous opportunity and a lifesaver. It was like a resurrection for me when my tutors allowed me to join their course, old as I was.

I think this is what our British-born young people need. You need that warm influence and inspiration to serve as a buffer against the negative influences that they get outside. You need to have that, especially nowadays.

Phyllis obtained a first-class honours degree in Caribbean Studies from London Metropolitan University when she was in her 70s, graduating in 2002. She now describes herself as a lifelong student of history, art and culture.

LINDA PRINCE

*From Jamaica, Linda's husband went to the UK to get
a job and settle in before sending for her in March 1957.*

D on't even begin to talk about the fog, that was
terrible! It was so thick that you couldn't even
see directly in front of where you were walking.
They had to get lanterns and guide them before the
buses so that people could get home from work in the
evenings, although it was bad in the mornings, too.

On top of that it was so cold, I am not telling you a
word of a lie. I never felt cold like that in my life. Back in
those days England was freezing. Chilblains used to eat
up your feet and your fingers 'til they turned purple and
black. It's true. It got so bad with me that they had to call
the doctor and he gave me some medicine and told me
to take bed rest because of the sores.

So now, I couldn't go to work. My husband prepared my breakfast, which was porridge, and when I got up I would just put the pot on top of the Beatrice Lamp (paraffin heater) to warm up, then eat the food and then go back to sleep. We passed through all that.

People who come to this country now have it good; we made it good for them because of all the hardships we endured and, believe you me, it was a real struggle in the olden days when I came to England in March 1957.

My husband came up in 1955 and then after he settled himself he paid the fare and sent for me. If I am truthful, I did not want to come because I had the children and my family all around me. But, the sad part about it is that I did love and miss my husband, Sonny, so there was nothing else for it.

I remember I wore a white organza dress, which was made for me by the dressmaker. In those days we would get our clothes made, especially for special occasions. Now, because we were going somewhere foreign, we really had to look good, so my dress was the business, I tell you. And then I had on a brown felt hat, which I wore skewed on the side of my head, brown spike heel shoes and gloves. We would always dress sprucey and nice back in those days, but when I arrived in this country and saw the fog and felt the cold I wanted to go straight back to Jamaica. It's a good job my husband came to meet me with the car and something warm to put 'round me.

I laugh about it now, but the first time I saw all the houses made of bricks, I thought they were churches because that is how the churches were built in Jamaica. I thought, "What a heap o' churches", but of course they were just ordinary houses.

The worse part about coming here at the beginning, apart from the cold, damp weather, was that I missed my children. I used to dream them all them time and in the dream I would beckon them to come but they couldn't come, so I was very sad.

I got a job straightaway and I remember one day I was crying at work —doing my job and crying at the same time — and the chargehand came up and asked me what was wrong. I told her I missed my family and she said, "Never mind, you will see them one day."

The only consolation, apart from being together with my husband again, was that I was a Christian and prayed that God would put me together with other believers, and that is what happened. The people we were living with (all except my husband, that is) were Christians. Brother and Sister Amos had the property and they used to keep prayer meetings in the house. Later on, they set up a church and community centre.

Church brethren were really like family. We lived good with one another and provided support for each other. Many of us are still in fellowship today, except for those who have passed away and gone on before.

I did a number of different jobs working in factories, hospitals, kitchens, even as a cashier, and eventually we were able to buy our own house and send for the children.

Through it all, the Pentecostal church was a big part of my life and that has not changed. I love to sing, dance and play my mouth-organ, praising the Lord.

One night, back in the old days, I was coming from church and a few of us decided to go and visit a church sister who was in hospital. We got a lift from a brother in his car, but I made the mistake of getting into the car and not shutting the door properly.

As the car turned the corner I fell out on the road, landing on my knees. It was only the grace of God that no vehicles were on the road, otherwise I could have been killed. I ended up in hospital, although they only treated me and sent me home. However, the damage was done because, apart from the pain in my body, I suffered a nervous breakdown and couldn't work like before. I was off work for a long time and then managed to go back part-time until eventually I retired. Now, I still suffer with pain from that accident.

When I look back, I have to thank God for keeping us and helping us make it in this country because it was a real struggle. My original plan to only come here for two years went right out the window. In fact, as we would say in Jamaica, "It melt like butter 'gainst sun", which is to say, my plans just dissolved. But, God is good — all the time.

HOME TO BRIXTON

*Donald Hinds' whimsical reminiscence of
Brixton, the black immigrants' "capital" during
the 1950s and '60s*

I lived in Brixton from 1956 to 1969. Eight years later, I returned to that town to teach British history to its sons, aged 11 to 18, at Tulse Hill comprehensive school.

The first headmaster of Tulse Hill School was a former deputy head of Dulwich public school. Tulse Hill was considered the working class students' public school. Its head boys wore gowns, and the masters attended assemblies in formal academic dress.

Although I have lived away from Brixton since 1969, the town which Brixi, the Anglo-Saxon, had marked out as his own territory — defining its northern boundary with a great stone — has never loosened its grip on me. It is that first passionate love thing.

Let me begin at the beginning. I got my first sight of Brixton on either the 23rd or 24th of August 1955. My mother and my stepfather had managed to get themselves re-housed by Southwark Council after my step-father had been duped into leasing a derelict building near Elephant and Castle.

He was anxious to provide suitable accommodation for his wife, my mother, who was due to arrive in London in late November 1951. The accommodation was a single bedroom flat, a sitting room/dining room and a kitchenette. There was a bath located under the kitchen table if one did not want to use the communal wash-room on the top floor.

There was a strict order that the flat was for a couple only, so I was registered as living at 3 Geneva Road, Brixton, and for the next year we worried about a late night inspection by the council acting on a tip-off from neighbours, but it never came.

I continued to sleep on the sofa, and all the documents which I had to present to employers and all who wished to see evidence of address were given that location as my place of abode in the Mother Country.

The room that my mother's friend shared with her boyfriend was crowded with suitcases and clothes hanging on rails, as if for them also that was not a place of permanent abode but a staging post to better accommodation. Perhaps this lady had obtained the room under strict agreement not to share, but share it she did.

Geneva Road was undoubtedly the slum capital of all slums, surpassing its neighbour, Somerleyton Road, which ran parallel. The streets had their backs turned to each other, like two contentious fish wives. Both adjoined Coldharbour Lane and provided entrances to Brixton Market and the Brixton Labour Exchange.

This guaranteed a noisy bustling surge of humanity between ten in the morning to five in the evening, giving a short respite before the pubs and the night clubs got into their swing.

Turning up at the Labour Exchange, I can still remember the excitement (or was it just confusion?) among the clerks when I presented my Jamaica Local Examination Certificate. There was excitement/confusion because they had never seen one before. However, eventually, the clerk suggested that I might wish to be tested for a job as a London Transport Executive Bus Conductor. It sounded very grand.

My boyhood dream of growing up and driving the most powerful American truck had not abandoned me. I had been on London buses in the few days since arriving from Jamaica, but had not seen any black conductors. Were I successful at the interview, I would not be driving an American truck or even a London bus, but conducting on one was the next best thing, or so I thought.

I was sent to the London Transport Recruitment Offices adjacent to Baker Street tube station. The preliminaries successfully cleared, a fortnight after training at Chiswick and later at Camberwell Garage, I was posted to Brixton London Transport Garage at Streatham Hill, where I was to become the fifth or sixth black bus conductor in the company. There, I was let loose on the already suspicious passengers who depended on routes 57, 95 and 109 on weekdays, and the 133 on Sundays. I remained in post from September 1955 until January 1965: exactly 9 years and 4 months.

For all that, I enjoyed my time on the buses. I was told some wonderful stories and even made some friends. I recall an old man, who might have been in his 80s, who told me that he could remember when there were verges on the roads (strips of grassland/vegetation), and that sheep were driven from the farms of Surrey to the slaughter house at Spitalfield Market *via* Brixton Hill. He also told me that Elizabeth the First came to Brixton in a boat leaving the Thames at Vauxhall and sailing up the Effra estuary when she visited Sir Walter Raleigh, whose residence was somewhere near Raleigh Gardens, a quarter of a mile from Lambeth Town Hall. Of course, none of these stories may have been true, but I was an impressionable colonial and enjoyed hearing such tales.

Within two weeks or so of starting work, the cleaner at the garage, a large old woman approached me in front of the other workers and announced that I reminded her of someone. I asked who and volunteered Harry Belafonte, whose handsome profile was seen in *Carmen Jones* and other films; or it might have been Frank Worrell, the immaculate cricket player. I went as far as to mention Paul Robeson, whose great voice and physique had been thrilling women and theatre-goers for decades. She shook her head in annoyance; she couldn't quite place who it was I was supposed to resemble.

A week or so slipped by before she broached the subject again. Then, one day she approached me with great elation. "I remember!" she shouted as she waddled closer to me.

"Really! Who is it?"

Divers and conductors gathered around for the great announcement.

"You remind me of the golliwog on Robertson strawberry jam jar!"

She delivered her statement with the timing of a music hall comic, and waddled off with her brush and cleaning bucket.

I do not recall any of the conductors and divers making any comments, neither did I, but it was years before I could face another jar of Robertson's jam.

Since there were few blacks (coloureds) behind the counters in shops and stores, I generally thought that the black bus conductors and underground workers were the acceptable face of black migrants. However, a daily uniform of clean shirt and tie and well-creased trousers rarely extracted a polite response from passengers, that being the British way.

But our presence was not lost on fellow immigrants, who would assume we knew of rooms to let, or how they could get to The Telephone Manufacturing Company or to PB Cow's of Streatham. Those were the two employers who had an insatiable need for immigrant labour.

As to accommodation, families were still sharing a single room and there were still stories of four or more men sharing. After flouting Southwark tenancy rules for nearly a year, my parents decided to buy their own house. As a family we took the upper floor and rented out the three available rooms on the ground floor to couples.

When my sister arrived in 1957, I declared my independence and found a room in Leander Road, Brixton Hill, which was a short walk to the bus garage where I worked. It was a spacious front room on the ground floor but had no other redeeming features.

I cooked on a gas ring which was placed in a metal tray, and the tattered cushions in the ancient wicker chairs were there to conceal the fact there were holes in the seats, which friends, who were in the habit of hurling rather than lowering themselves onto chairs, would discover to their cost.

There were also two single beds which creaked and that was the contents of the room. The weekly rent was two pounds ten shillings. My weekly pay was a few pence short of eight pounds.

Brixton market was like the proverbial Piccadilly Circus: busy and noisy. If you ventured among its stalls long enough, you would be sure to meet a cousin or a friend you thought was still in Jamaica; or you could quite possibly bump into someone who wanted to know if you knew of a room for rent or if you wanted to rent a room in a nice house.

A bus ride from the centre of Brixton there were enough cinemas to take your mind off the old black and white television where racist jokes were completely the norm:

"I say, I say, if the black postman delivers the mail at night would it be blackmail?"
"I say, I say, how does the Arab make love?"
"I don't know, how does the Arab make love?"
"In tents! Boo-boom."

There were four cinemas within the shopping district: the ABC next to the Town Hall, the Astoria at the beginning of Stockwell Road and the Pullman almost adjoining The Tate Library. Its winter slogan to entice customers was *"It's warmer inside!"* This was changed at the start of summer to: *"Its cooler inside!"*

I recall once seeing a long queue hoping to get in to see an x-rated French film. In front of me were two young lads. The cashier took one look at the youngest one and said "Sorry, lad, you cannot go in, you don't look 18." Whereupon the lad pulled a birth certificate from his inside jacket pocket and shoved it across to the woman to prove her wrong. She didn't bother with the other one.

There was also the Empress Theatre (later to become the Granada) behind Morley's department store. A bus stop from the Town Hall was the Clifton, which seemed to specialise in old Westerns. Further afield there was a forgotten cinema at Herne Hill and another at Stockwell.

There was what seemed like an endless stream of black entrepreneurs who made several attempts at operating clubs only to have them closed as quickly by the police. However, there were what appeared to be weekly birth night celebrations of ageless matriarchs. It was curious that these were never birthday celebrations, neither did they celebrate men's birth nights. These parties were patronised by about ten men to every female.

Parties were usually held in the front room on the ground floor. There was hardly any room for jiving because of how closely packed the floor was, but it was an excuse for bodies touching in an exaggerated form of the rumba.

We smooched to Billy Ecksteine and Sarah Vaughan, and Shirley and Lee; and jived to jazz rhythms, and to Antonio 'Fats' Domino's *Blue Berry Hill* and Lloyd Prices' *Staggerlee*; and mentoes and calypsos *Trek to England* and *Banana, Banana Banana!*

Back on the platform of the buses, there were queries from black passengers as to where to find Theo's Record Shop, *The West Indian Gazette* newspaper, the Black Law Firm, and last but not least the estate agent — Ross & Ross — which acted on behalf of blacks buying a house. That was easy: they were all located along Brixton Road, three of them at number 250, where Theo's Record shop occupied the ground floor, The *West Indian Gazette*, the floor above, and the law firm, the top floor.

Theo Campbell's record shop might have been the first black-operated record shop in London. Theo, who was always immaculately presented from head to shoes, also possessed an encyclopaedic knowledge of American jazz and popular music.

The *West Indian Gazette* was the first black commercial newspaper. By that I mean it was not the mouthpiece of an organisation. It actually could be bought at most newsstands for a sixpence. It was edited by Claudia Jones, who was born in Trinidad and migrated with her family to Harlem in 1923, and was radicalised by the position of blacks in the USA. She was eventually deported to London in 1955.

I joined the paper's list of enthusiastic writers in June 1958, although I was still a London Transport bus conductor, who also did the occasional broadcast for the BBC's

Caribbean Service.

On the *Gazette*, we covered the Notting Hill riots; the outcry of the tenants of the Rachman estates, the Rivona Trials, which showed the calibre of men like Nelson Mandela and Robert Sobukwe in South Africa's incredibly long walk to freedom.

Turning to the Arts, we celebrated the novels of Caribbean writers Jan Carew, George Lamming, VS Naipaul, Samuel Selvon, Andrew Salkey and others. From this corner of Brixton we sometimes met artistes at the newly-opened Indian restaurant, the Taj Mahal in Vining Street, to discuss the careers of entertainers such as Edric and Pearl Connor, Basco Holder, Pearl Prescod, Roy Henry, Nadia Catouse, Cy Grant, Sylvia Winter and many others.

We even dared to set up London's first Caribbean Carnival. OK, so it was at St Pancras Town Hall, which was not exactly Rio or Port of Spain. There were six carnivals in all from January 1959 to April 1964.

Modern critics are saying a town hall is nowhere for a carnival. My answer is this: The Mighty Sparrow crowned it with a spectacular performance in 1962 at Seymour Hall — therefore, it was a carnival!

REMEMBERING COLUMBUS

A tribute to Oswald "Columbus" Denniston, who travelled to Britain on the SS Empire Windrush in 1948.

To traders and shoppers in Brixton market he was something of an institution. Columbus, the fabric seller with the heart of gold, would regale young and old alike with his charm, humour and generosity.

He was lauded as the man who had smashed a bigoted cartel that prohibited blacks from trading in Brixton market to become, it is claimed, the first African-Caribbean stall holder trading there.

Columbus, who died in February 2000, was a businessman in his Jamaica homeland and had travelled widely before embarking on that iconic Windrush voyage to England in the years following the war.

En route, he had displayed his business acumen by leaving the ship at one of its stop-offs and returned with watermelons, which he cut up and sold to passengers. The gesture earned him the nickname, "Columbus", which stuck so fast that few people ever actually knew his real name. Fellow Windrush passenger Sam King later paid tribute to the long-suffering businessman by relating the immense hardships he encountered and surmounted in trying to set up in business during the 1950s.

According to Mr King, having secured a stall in Brixton market, which at that time was allegedly run like a mafia operation by certain traders who didn't like "outsiders", Columbus was threatened with bicycle chains and knee-capping after his first day of trading there.

Undaunted, he returned the threats and found himself fighting off attacks from those who did not want "his kind" working there as traders. By standing his ground and setting up shop in the south London market, Columbus opened the doors to many other business men and women from diverse backgrounds.

Born in 1913, and credited as "an unselfish and determined man", he was also described variously as "a bit of a diplomat"; a "calming influence who always had something constructive to contribute", and "a man who made time for people". At the time of Columbus' memorial, fellow business pioneer Len Dyke (himself now deceased) related a story told to him by Columbus in which the trader had given his young assistant instructions about how to pack away the rolls of fabrics from the market stall after the day's trading.

There were strict orders that the rolls of black cloth were to be placed on the bottom of the pile. However, the assistant angrily refused to obey, challenging the notion that "blacks are always on the bottom".

Rather than force a confrontation, the boss relented. His own experience of racism and injustice made him understand the young man's point of view. Columbus allowed him to load the cart with the black fabric taking pride of place on the top. The analogy struck a chord.

TWO DAYS IN APRIL
Z. Nia Reynolds

Two days in April 1968. Two men: one Black, one White. One had a dream, the other, a nightmare. Martin Luther King was the dreamer, who envisioned a brotherhood of man where racial hatred was extinct. Enoch Powell, a political Cassandra, had an apparition of "Rivers of Blood" if Britain admitted "unchecked numbers" of dark-skinned people from its colonies into the country.

On the 4th April 1968, an assassin's bullet ripped through the throat of the dreamer, shattering the vocal cords of the peacemaker who had uttered one of the greatest speeches of the twentieth century. A man who spoke truth to power.

This was the man who advocated non-violence, who had the courage to visualize a world in which people would be judged, not on the basis of the colour of their skin, but by "the content of their character", and who had the eloquence and charisma to transmit that hope to millions across the globe.

On the 20th April 1968, Enoch Powell, the

Conservative Member of Parliament, foreshadowed racial conflict arising from Black immigration. Many had thought it, whispered it over their pints in pubs and over their fences while hanging out laundry; had muttered their concerns between gritted teeth during tea breaks on the job, while waiting for buses and trains, while at the grocer's, or wherever they caught sight of the Outsiders: those "presumptuous dark interlopers".

Only Powell had dared to give it loud, open voice, boldly from the podium, not whimperingly from the shadows like a man afraid to speak up in his own house.

To Powell and those who shared his fears, Black immigrants, who were arriving in Britain in "uncontrolled numbers" at the risk of "swamping" indigenous Britons, were coming, not to make a contribution and slot into a society they already knew so much about as subjects of its Empire, they were coming to cause mayhem.

To these antagonists, the immigrants had the temerity to call themselves "British" and were flaunting their British citizenship and British passports, rights accorded them by the Nationality Act. Instead, they were deemed a menace and harbingers of doom and disruption, although some conceded that they may well have "helped out" during the two world wars.

The colonies had supported the war efforts and had sent supplies, and many had risked their lives signing up and crossing treacherous waters loaded with German subs to reach Britain and Europe. Some had even died for that cause. But, now that the war was over and victory won, there was a sense of "that was then, this is now". Certain foreigners were no longer welcome, even if they were still needed.

Post-war Britain did need rebuilding and required the incoming labour, but many immigrants were met with an attitude that enquired: "did so many have to come?" And "why were they so intent on staying?"

At the time of Powell's speech, Kelso Cochrane was long dead, having been murdered by racist thugs in West London in 1959, although no one had, or has ever been prosecuted for the crime.

Powell's speech was significant because it was seen as powerful enough to fuel the fire of fear and hatred that had perpetrated such violence in the first place.

Just 16 days separated the murder of Martin Luther King and Enoch Powell's Rivers of Blood speech. Although distant in terms of location, it is hard not to think of the two acts as monumental for the sheer scale and scope of their resonance, dissonance and eloquence.

They said to one another, "Here comes that dreamer. Come, let us kill him…then we will see what comes of his dreams."

King's assassination was devastating and sent shock waves around the world, while Powell's speech also had the impact of an assassin's bullet. Yet a chasm separated them because those who dared to believe it knew, deep in their hearts, that a murderer's bullet may have killed Martin Luther King, the dreamer, but his prophecy could still be fulfilled.

And they also knew that Enoch Powell's nightmare of racial conflict could only be achieved if enough good people surrendered to the fear that could fan that hatred into flame. Thankfully, that was not to be.

It is a long, arduous and continuous journey towards inclusion and equality, but there is hope that Britain will eventually celebrate its diversity much more tangibly than just in its love of chicken tikka masala and jerk chicken.

Perhaps it will happen in the way that Martin Luther King prescribed: "We must learn to live together as brothers, or are we going to perish together as fools?"

"A people without the knowledge of its past history,
origin and culture, is like a tree without roots."

– Marcus Garvey

Sankofa: "Go back and take it".

Arrival Hall
Immigration Archive

Advertising poster for BWIA   *WICTE exhibition*

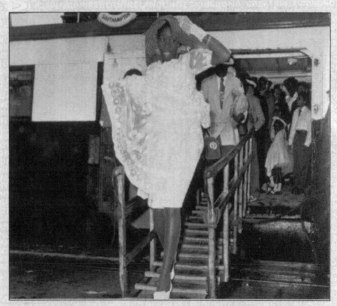

Young woman arrives at Southampton in the 1960s.
Immigration Archive

Disembarking at Southampton.
Immigration Archive

Bus ticket from the 1950s & '60s
when bus fares costs pennies.
Black Stock Archive

One pound note - legal tender in the 1950s. '60s & '70s.
Black Stock Archive

Early street carnival.
WICTE exhibition

Journey of a lifetime? West Indians arrive in England.
Immigration Archive

Mother and child arrive in England on a rainy morning.
Immigration Archive

Studio portrait to
send "back home".
WICTE exhibition

Nurse Patterson
*Photo: ©Winnifred Byer
/ Black Stock Archive*

Susan Ricketts
Photo: ©Susan Ricketts / Black Stock Archive

Winnifred Byer
Photo: ©Winnifred Byer / Black Stock Archive

Hazel Walcott
©Hazel Walcott / Black Stock Archive

Clive & Little Gloria, '60s singing duo
©Gloria Browne / Black Stock Archive

Rennie Miller
Photo: ©Rennie Miller /
Black Stock Archive

Susan Ricketts
Photo: ©Susan Ricketts
/ Black Stock Archive

WEST INDIAN GAZETTE

and Afro-Asian-Caribbean News

VOL. 3. NO. 6. APRIL 1961   ALL THE NEWS YOU WANT FROM HOME AND HERE   6d.

LADBROKE GROVE PUB COLOUR-BAR

ARCHIE SPENCER, Jamaican-born barman was the victim of a colour bar experience when recently he went into a Ladbroke Grove public house, asked for a glass of bitter and was told that "we don't serve coloured people here."

After this experience, he told the story to a group of friends who then arranged a mixed party of coloured and white persons to visit the pub last night.

The three white people went in and sat down drinking when there were several other white persons in the pub. Five minutes after, three coloured followed, two men and a girl from Ghana, and asked to be served. They were told curtly "We don't serve you people here."

When asked by one of the fellows, "what do you mean by this?" Came the reply, "In other words we don't serve coloured people in this pub."

The Ghana girl also stood for a minute and was told "we have trouble with them." Then she asked "don't you have trouble with the English people, then?" The reply was "this is my pub and I serve who I want to serve here and please get out."

Mr. Paul Du Preez, one of the white persons in the party that...

MBOYA WINS IN KENYA ...

Dr. Kiano Rejoices In Triumph over Kenya

CHERRY LARMAN, 19 year-old student nurse from Jamaica, gets a kiss of congratulations while being presented by Mr. Rex Boultinghorpe, Acting Commissioner for the West Indies, British Guiana and British Honduras at WIG'S Third Caribbean Carnival at Mecca Locarno in February. 1960 Queen Marlene Walker looks on. (Story — Page 5 Other Photos — Page 7).

WEST INDIAN GAZETTE

AND AFRO-ASIAN CARIBBEAN NEWS

VOL. 5. No. 11 JUNE, 1963   Price 6d.   250 Brixton Road, London, N.W.9.   'Phone: BRI 1734

Negro People in U.S.A. Mount Struggles to End Jim Crow

CRISIS GROWS IN BRITISH GUIANA

SHORTAGES of essential foods like sugar, flour, milk, cooking oil and margarine are becoming acute in British Guiana. The country remains in the grip of a seven-week-old general strike and lock-out called by the Trades Union Council.

The Labour legislation introduced by the P.P.P. Government (see page 3) on June 2, the same Trades Union Council who called the strike, against the B.G. Government of "putting pressure on the strikers to cause an eruption of violence from which the People's Progressive Party would gain.

But many observers took the "facing both ways" approach as a sign that the Trades Union Council is not so sure of its ground.

Observers were also wondering why, in view of Mr Frank Cousins' absence and several others of his trip...

STOP PRESS

The organisers of the Daily Mirror Caribbean Carnival on June 29th, regret that owing to circumstances beyond their control, they have been obliged to cancel the Carnival. All monies will be automatically refunded.

NO one, who has watched the superb struggle of the Negro people in Birmingham, Alabama, and its spread to more than 43 southern cities, can fail to recognise that what we are witnessing is a new leap in their freedom struggle. They fight to win for themselves and their children elementary democratic rights which they have long been denied.

In a counter-reply the Birmingham authorities, "guardians" of white supremacy, now crumbling under the hammer blows of the united Negro people's freedom demands. These backward practitioners of racialism seek to rely on the use of terror to frighten the freedom fighters. They have called into use their Police Dogs; their powerful jet Fire Hoses; they have engaged in indiscriminate beatings of women and children; they fill their jails to overflowing with thousands of protesting men, women and children; they bomb and burn the homes of Negro leaders; they sjambok the children from school.

BUT THE NEGRO PEOPLE FIGHT ON! THEY SING THEIR FREEDOM SONGS: "WE WILL OVERCOME"!

Their superb spirit is reflected in the mouth of babes. Like the little girl, starched and prim, calling impatiently to her schoolmate, "Harry up, Lucille, or you'll be late to go to jail!"

Mirrored in the Birmingham Negro freedom struggle is the impact of the denial of elementary...

That inferior citizenship status was openly admitted recently by a Civil Rights Commission of the U.S. Department of Justice.

"Although the whites are not immune, Negroes feel the brunt of official brutality proportionately more than any other group in America."

Copies of the groundbreaking West Indian Gazette newspaper
Black Stock Archive

Josephine Matticks
©*Josephine Matticks / Black Stock Archive*

To those whose stories have been told,
And those whose stories will yet be told;
To those who know that the half
has never yet been told.

— *Thank you.*